W9-DIT-356

VICTORIAN CORNERS

BY THE SAME AUTHOR

VICTORIANA

Victorian Furniture (1952); *The Victorian Child* (1959); *Home Furnishing with Antiques* (includes Victoriana, 1965)

ANTIQUE FURNITURE

English Period Furniture: An Introductory Guide (1946); *Old English Furniture from Tudor to Regency* (1948); *English Cottage Furniture* (1949; 3rd, revised, ed., 1961); *Windsor Chairs* (1953).

ART AND ARTISTS

Henry Bright of the Norwich School (1920); *Charles Bentley, O.W.S.* (1921); *Dictator of the Royal Academy* (1921); *David Cox* (1924); *Sporting Prints of the 18th and early 19th Centuries* (1927); *Catalogue of Paintings and Drawings in the F. J. Nettlefold Collection* (with C. Reginald Grundy, 1937–38); *Etty and the Nude* (with William Gaunt, 1943); *The Nude from Cranach to Etty and beyond* (1944); *Cox the Master* (1946); *Rowlandson* (1947); *Sea Painters of Britain* (1947–48); *The British Museum's Pictures* (with J. R. Fawcett Thompson, 1961).

VARIOUS

Coronation Cavalcade (1937); *The Life and Times of King Edward VIII* (1937); *The Bronze Cross* (1945); *Clarence below the Basement* (for children, 1948); *Britain's Birthright* (1950); *The Georgian Child* (companion to *The Victorian Child*, 1961).

In The Queen's Shadow: a white-ware Staffordshire group commemorating the marriage (1871) of Queen Victoria's 4th daughter, HRH The Princess Louise to John (Campbell), Marquess of Lorne, later 9th Duke of Argyll. (*Mr and Mrs Michael Maynard*)

VICTORIAN CORNERS

The Style and Taste of an Era

BY F. GORDON ROE

with illustrations by
Frances Maynard and others

FREDERICK A. PRAEGER, *Publishers*

New York Washington

BOOKS THAT MATTER

Published in the United States of America in 1969
by Frederick A. Praeger, Inc., Publishers
111 Fourth Avenue, New York, N.Y. 10003

Library of Congress Catalog Card Number: 78-79072

Printed in Great Britain

For Frances and Michael
with love

CONTENTS

ILLUSTRATIONS

PLATES

IN THE TEXT

Note:—Uncaptioned tailpieces are from *The Child's Companion for 1841*.

FOREWORD

THIS book is less of a guide than a background to the collecting of Victoriana. To study things without reference to the settings for which they were meant is to miss much of the point and a good deal of the fun. Likewise, in assessing Victorian art one needs to know something of Victorian artists and their ways of thought, whatever be their status in the taste of the moment.

And here, in fairness to myself, I declare that I do not necessarily share every opinion *quoted* in this book. Nor do I necessarily *like* everything which comes into my theme. Experience has taught me that there is, here and there, always a reader disposed to interpret a 'mention' as implying admiration of the mentioned by an author who may utterly loathe it. They are so mistaken. To put it bluntly, I have written in this book of persons and things I admire, and of persons and things in whose company I would not choose to be found dead. If at times my personal opinion bursts through, I have tried to be fair and to give, as far as it goes, an unbiased sketch of such aspects of the changing Victorian scene as may help to place a would-be collector or student 'in the picture'.

F. Gordon Roe

Alexandra Park
London, N.22

ACKNOWLEDGMENT

FOR personal advice or assistance I am valuably indebted to Mr Claude Blair, FSA, Mr Adrian Bury, RWS, Mr W. G. Campbell, ALA (Reference Librarian, Hornsey Central Library), Mr John Newton Chance, Mr Peter Desborough, Sir William Russell Flint, RA, P/PRWS, Mr John Gloag, FSA, HON. ARIBA, Mrs Dorothy Green, ALA, Mr Sidney C. Hutchison, MVO, FSA (Librarian, Royal Academy of Arts), Mr Derek Lewis (Gramophone Librarian, BBC), Miss Cecelia Neville, Mr L. G. G. Ramsey, FSA (Editor, *The Connoisseur*), Mr Robert Rowe, FMA (Director, Temple Newsom House, Leeds), Mr and Mrs A. Spencer, Mr George L. Suckling, Mr J. R. Fawcett Thompson, Mr Reginald Williams (Department of Prints and Drawings, British Museum), Mr T. A. Walden (Director) and Mr L. S. Lambourne (Keeper of Art, City of Leicester Museums and Art Gallery), Miss M. E. Weaver, AMA (Deputy Borough Curator, Walthamstow); the Libraries of the British Museum, the Victoria and Albert Museum, the Alexandra Park Branch Library, and the Reference Librarian, Church End Branch Library, Finchley, for data concerning The Avenue. My indebtedness to my father, the late Fred Roe, RI, is apparent. My daughter, Frances Maynard, has contributed ideas as well as illustrations; and I am grateful, too, to my wife Eleanor, and my son-in-law Michael Maynard.

Besides books elsewhere mentioned, the following are among those consulted: Algernon Graves's *The Royal Academy Exhibitors*; Holbrook Jackson's *The Eighteen Nineties*; George Sampson's *Concise History of English Literature*; Gleeson White's *Ballades and Rondeaus* (Canterbury Poets); T. Martin Wood's *George du Maurier*; the Histories of *Punch* by M. H. Spielmann (1895) and R. G. G. Price (1957); Thomas Balston's *Staffordshire Portrait Figures of the Victorian Age* (1958) and *Supplement* (1963); Geoffrey A. Godden's *Victorian Porcelain* (1961); R. W. Symonds and B. B. Whineray's *Victorian Furniture* (1962). Brian Reade's *Aubrey Beardsley*, and his and Frank Dickinson's Catalogue of the *Aubrey Beardsley Exhibition at the Victoria and Albert Museum* (both 1966) are important additions to Beardsleyana. C. Reginald Grundy's own annotated copy of Graves's *Dictionary of Artists* has been useful; as have the *D.N.B.*, *Who was Who* (*v.y.*), and *Thieme-Becker*. Some passages from my own articles in *The Connoisseur* on 'The Lighter Side of Collecting' (1941) are, with permission, adapted to the present account of Victorian comics; and a correspondence on 'Ally Sloper' in the *Daily Telegraph* (1966) has been noted. Should any due acknowledgment have been overlooked, I trust that the lapse will be excused.

F. G. R.

ONE

From Dowdy to Antique

'Unborn To-morrow, and dead Yesterday.' EDWARD FITZGERALD

I

At precisely 6.30 in the evening of Tuesday, January 22, 1901, my china mug, with its insipidly coloured head of Queen Victoria amidst the drooping flags of Empire, entered obsolescence. Admittedly the Diamond Jubilee, for which that mug was made, was a mere four years ago and things were not easily outdated, especially in the nursery. It took a cataclysm to dowse the fairy lamps of 1897, and in that January cataclysm broke. The Old Queen was dead at last.

Seen or invisible, her presence had been taken for granted; the world had long since grown used to her. She had become that most venerated of Britain's household gods – an institution. And now nothing remained but to bury her with pomp, to acclaim her successor, and to carry on confidently as befitted membership of an Empire on which the sun, by no stretch of the imagination, could ever set.

Such was the general idea, though the amazing fact that there was no longer a Queen Victoria took a deal of getting used to. It was as though one were suddenly told that the Great Sphinx at Giza had died in its sleep.

Not that, in those days, I was aware of the Great Sphinx; but I *was* aware of Queen Victoria, and, in a childish way, supposed her to be a friend of the family. There on my night-nursery mantelshelf, balancing a photograph of my Grannie Lee in a stylish dress of the middle '80s, was a staring commercial portrait of the Queen, presumably cut from the lid of a chocolate box. How this, far from the most beguiling of royal *effigies*, came into my nursery at all is immaterial, though my governess, who (bless her!) took in a religious weekly and revered the good and great, may have been involved.

Anyhow, there on the mantelshelf was the Queen herself, globe-eyed and bejewelled. Her crowned VR cypher was still plain to see on every pillar-box. Her head still graced coinage and postage stamps. The Empire (on which the sun never set) was still red on maps of the world. And a small boy went on drinking his milk from his Diamond Jubilee mug, with the dead Queen's head on it.

Until, that is, a rival mug appeared on the nursery table: a rival gradually accepted. Instead of one royal head, this intruder bore two, less anaemic in colour. To my left, a full-favoured gentleman with neatly trimmed beard, and a bravely decorated scarlet tunic, crossed by the blue riband of the Garter; to my right, a gracious lady, her dark hair fashionably frizzed and tiara'd, and about her throat a choker of pearls. Both heads reflected the frozen air of official portraiture. One had to remind oneself that these Olympians were no

Fig. 1. 'In a stylish dress of the middle '80s', here framed *à l'Art Nouveau*

longer Prince and Princess of Wales, but King Edward VII and Queen Alexandra. Their Majesties!

2

Thus it was that my Diamond Jubilee mug entered its decline. For a while, it shared place with its brighter-hued rival; but a day came when it was banished to the limbo of crockery stored in a basement china-cupboard. There, cracked and uncared for, it languished until, years later, my Mother, busy 'turning out', found that mug and asked me whether I wouldn't like to keep it? But no. I was grown-up, intolerant; my mood was for antiques; the mug was 'merely Victorian', and no good at that. I was high-and-mightily dismissive – and now regret it. . . .

3

Before anyone accuses me of nostalgia, it should be made clear that the tale of my Diamond Jubilee mug is introduced here with a purpose. In its own small way, it is a microcosm of a process familiar enough to collectors. Things are new and (maybe) modish; they become old and dowdy. Antiques they are not, just old-fashioned, so out with them! For a while, perhaps for a long while, they survive in the limbo of the obsolete. Then, *something* – the passing of time, a veer of taste, a revival of interest, a sudden topicality, even an organized manœuvre by interested parties – and the scene is transformed. Things which till then, and whatever their original merit or status, could be scarcely given away, are searched out, regarded with a nostalgic respect or an aesthetic enthusiasm which may or may not be justified by facts. And the price of the hitherto unsaleable rises accordingly.

Meanwhile, throughout all such vicissitudes, the objects concerned, whatever they may be,

1. *Honeywood introducing the Bailiffs to Miss Richland as his friends:* a scene from Goldsmith's play, *The Good-natur'd man* (1767) as interpreted by *W. P. Frith* (1850) (*Sheepshanks Gift—Victoria and Albert Museum*)

2. Typical of the large engravings with which many Victorians plastered their walls: *There's Life in the Old Dog Yet!* by C. A. Tomkins after Sir Edwin Landseer. (*British Museum*)

In white, with a spray of scarlet blooms . . . Fred Roe's portrait of *Mabel, daughter of Sydney W. Lee, Esqre.*, in the Royal Academy, 1889.

Fig. 2. Young Britain: after a coloured-litho from a Victorian scrap-book. (*Mr Winslow Rhode*)

and excluding the fragmentary or 'adapted', *are still the same objects*. It is we, not they who are changed; nor can we flatter ourselves in a backhanded way as iconoclasts. A like process of demotion and rehabilitation has been going on, and off, for ages. Modish Victoriana from the beginning of the reign in 1837 are not the same as modish Victoriana from its close in 1901 – bearing in mind that these are *historical*, not *stylistic*, dates which may very well differ materially. No new style sprang into being in 1837; no style was abruptly cut short in 1901. Thus if, in what follows, I stray here and there in an attractive (though relevant) byway, it will be without heeding the potential disfavour of those whose literary flights are bounded by historical tables and dictionaries. Sir Compton Mackenzie wrote in *The Queen's House*: 'the dead hand of late Victorianism was to lie heavily upon the country for a lustrum and to youth the new century did not seem to begin until January, 1906'.[1]

That was not quite my own impression, coloured as mine was by a house-moving in 1904; but the fact remains that Victorianism, if dead and dowdy, did not finally collapse until 1914. Even now, faint signs of movement may be detected, as a kind of faintly lingering tradition: 'the thoughts of vanished men, which still haunted rather than participated in the world of to-day', to borrow an apt phrase from H. G. Wells. Such tradition, which I regard as distinct from the neo-Victorian revival, has much to commend it and is now discerning a merit in assorted Victoriana.

All the same, and to make a workable proposition of my text, it is largely matters arising between 1837 and 1901 with which this book is concerned. The which brings one to an obvious, if not invariably digested detail that by no means all Victoriana are in any strict sense 'antique'. Not yet, at any rate, though Time will see to that.

For general purposes, an antique is deemed to have at least a century of age behind it; which means in effect that, at the time of writing, somewhere about half of the Victorian Age qualifies through its surviving products.

4

But, as already hinted, Time rolls on, and the general attrition of antiquities is compensated by admissions to the fold. Whether 'new' entrants are invariably as interesting, as important, as qualitatively or quantitatively desirable as their predecessors in the antiquarian elysium, must be decided in specific cases. Not so long ago, almost all Victoriana were airily dismissed as dowdy, fit for the dustbin or its competitor the junk-shop. Now many such things are in danger of being over-esteemed for supposedly aesthetic qualities which, in sundry instances, they are far from possessing. To plumb the vast depth of Victoriana in a single volume is impossible; so what I propose is no social history as such, no painfully argued *excursus* on arts and crafts, no learnedly annotated catalogue, neatly ranged from A–Z – such works exist already, and will assuredly be followed by others. There are moments when one cannot see the trees for the wood.

Wherefore, I invite my readers to poke around with me in Victorian corners, singling out here a memorable artist or a famous picture, here (because it suits our mood) a less important one; there anything from a designer to a sideboard, a desk, a dish, a hair-tidy, a brooch or a bracelet – or even a yellowing 'comic' long since thrown away by some old boy who, in latter age, would have given his ears for another sight of it.

In this spirit then, let us start our Victorian quest with a glance at selected aspects of Victorian painting.

[1] (Sir) Compton Mackenzie: *The Queen's House/A History of Buckingham Palace* (Hutchinson), p. 31.

TWO

Of Victorian Painting (A Sketch)

'Mind what you say, my dear!' her aunt interposed. 'It's by an R.A.!'
LEWIS CARROLL

I

BUT what *is* Victorian Painting? Nowadays, this label is applied not so much to the whole enormous mass of work produced between 1837–1901, plus its heralds and hang-overs, as to certain trends within it: trends for the most part distinguished by a high degree of technical efficiency and thematic content, steeped in an unmistakably Victorian mood. If too narrow, this popular conception of 'Victorian art' is not irrelevant, as is demonstrated by posing the question: not *what* are Victorian paintings, but *who* were 'Victorian' painters?

J. M. W. Turner (born back in 1775) lived on into 1851, the year of the Great Exhibition, but, taken in the mass, his art is no more 'Victorian' than it is 'Georgian' or 'Regency'. It is 'Turner', for which no synonym exists. That is the one great, overriding fact, before which stylistic and dynastic symbols pale. (Parenthetically, just why, of late years, Turner should have been represented in some quarters as a 're-discovered' master, is beyond my comprehension. When I was a boy well over fifty years ago, Turner was being celebrated both critically and in such popular works as the familiar *Masterpieces in Colour* series and *Bell's Miniature Series of Painters*, which, as the saying goes, went everywhere. But that is by the way.)

2

When Turner died, his vacant place in the ranks of Royal Academicians was eventually filled by the election of William Powell Frith, who, unlike Turner, can be reasonably classed as a Victorian painter. This is no mere matter of dates, even though Frith (1819–1909) was born in the same year as the Queen, and did all his most significant painting in that long reign of hers. What really tells is that, to a great extent in mood and perhaps even more so in technique, his art aligns with an unmistakably Victorian phase of thought. The difference between Turner and Frith is the difference between genius and high talent. If (in the words of Oliver Onions) 'Nothing in art can be produced without prayer and fasting – not even obscenity', it follows that paint so free of all offence as Frith's immensely capable performance is, within his talent's limitations, very talented indeed. Whistler's bitter gibe after Frith had given evidence against him in the 'Pot-of-Paint' trial of 1878 demonstrates how poles apart the two men were, and not in art alone. It was (Frith had said somewhere) a toss-up whether he became an artist or an auctioneer, to which Whistler in *The Gentle Art of Making Enemies* (1890) appended the comment: 'he must have tossed-up'. But if Frith was wrong about Whistler, we may fairly claim in a longer perspective that Whistler was wrong about Frith.

Even if we look no further than his two best-remembered works, *The Derby Day* (1858) and, freer in touch, *The Railway Station* (1862), we are compelled to recall the name of Frith at once. Nobody else could have painted them as he painted them, and nobody else could paint them in just that way nowadays. They are 'Frith', but they are also immensely 'Victorian', and vastly informative about Victorian England.

Of course, there were always those who found fault with *The Derby Day*. Even John Leech, who was Frith's friend, had a bad word for it. 'Not a bit like life. Swell in black trousers', said Leech. Even so, to adopt a more recent expression, both *The Derby Day* and *The Railway Station* were 'raves' in their own day. Here was popular art (not 'pop art', please) *in excelsis*.

On the opening day of the Royal Academy Summer Exhibition of 1858, a policeman had to be stationed to keep back the crowd from *The Derby Day*, and, a few days later, an iron crush-rail was erected in front of the picture. Since the Academy was founded in 1768, this was only the second time that such a precaution was taken; and it was by no means the last on which Frith's work was so complimented.

But excitement waned though the subject of *The Derby Day* always attracted interest; its mood and treatment slowly became old-fashioned, quite marvellously done but (as some put it) a 'type of a time'. It entered the phase of the curious. Mr Frith, now aged but still painting, and sometimes repeating earlier successes, was treated with the respect due to a famous old man.

This stage had already been reached when that Diamond Jubilee mug of mine was still in use. Even so, there were always those who (maybe with more respect than admiration) recognized Frith's peculiar ability. And, in due season, long after its ancient creator was dead, folk rather slowly began to see *The Derby Day*, *The Railway Station*, as well as the *Ramsgate Sands* (of 1854) and other performances in a new light: a light undistorted by sensationalism, topicality, aesthetic tyrannies or the dread of being thought dowdy. In short, they looked for themselves, and began to see William Powell Frith as what he in fact was: a 'little master'; and to be a little master is in itself an outstanding achievement.

3

By one of those chances that make life interesting, Frith and my parents moved, he from Bayswater to St John's Wood, they from Chelsea to West Hampstead, at much about the same time; we in 1898, he a shade earlier. This not in itself very memorable fact was one of the causes of a friendship arising between Fred Roe, my father, a much younger painter, and the venerable artist of *The Derby Day* fame. About 1899 is an approximate date, as being that on the earliest letters we had from him, which have survived.

Mr Frith, in his tall hat or square bowler, would toddle round from his house on Clifton Hill for a chat and a mild cigar. And, one day, Fred Roe who had bought a copy of Frith's book *My Autobiography and Reminiscences*, asked him if he would inscribe it. Frith said he would take it away with him. When the book came back, it was not merely inscribed, but carried a lengthy message in its author's own hand. I may be excused for quoting this hitherto unpublished gem:

'Clifton Hill Dec. 1 1900

'I have read this book with much pleasure & some surprise on finding that the author – whose pictures I cannot admire – has altogether mistaken his true vocation. As a writer few can surpass him, as a painter he is in my opinion very mediocre indeed. My friend Mr. F. Roe has paid me the compliment of asking my opinion of these reminiscences & here it is.'

'WP. Frith'

'I may be permitted to express a hope that my friend Roe will prove a better painter than the author of this book, otherwise he will have a poor chance of a niche in the Temple of Fame.'

As from a famous elder to a rising man, what could be more courteous and charming? One feels that the words he himself had had bestowed on him as a young man by the great Turner were not forgotten.

Nor is this the lone instance, within my knowledge, of Frith's kindly spirit. When, in the afterwash of the bitter feeling aroused by the secession of what became the Meyrick Society from the old Kernoozers' Club, Roe found himself estranged from one of his most valued professional friends, it was Frith who took the first step to aid a reconciliation which eventually, and happily, followed. 'I hear from Mr Frith' [everyone called him 'Mr' Frith] wrote Estranged Friend to Roe, 'that you have an important work for the approaching Academy, and would like to come and see it.' That was all, and it worked. Very neat, Mr Frith!

Clearly, about this time, Roe had made something of a confidant of the distinguished old man, for when, in the December of 1901, he suffered the shock of losing his mother, a note went out to Mr Frith. Back came an immediate, gentle reply in which figured the words: 'I still remember my own grief when my mother died just fifty years ago.'[2]

4

The names of Frith and Sir Edwin Landseer are in the van of those whom one thinks of when 'Victorian' painting is mooted. There are plenty of others; but, even with the worst of intentions, Landseer is inescapable.

Here is another artist of outstanding talent, whose paint, having scaled the heights and sounded the deeps of critical and popular praise and contempt, came into his own again nearly ninety years after his death. From being immensely revered, his status declined until to mention, say, *The Stag at Bay* or *The Monarch of the Glen* was to imply one's whimsical sense of outmoded absurdity. At last came the rehabilitation, crowned by the Landseer Exhibition, held in the Royal Academy's Diploma Gallery in 1961. It then again became obvious (as some had already risked ridicule by asserting) that Landseer was capable of

[2] A. L. S., W. P. Frith to Fred Roe, December 17 [1901]. *In the Author's possession.* Maria, Mrs Robert Roe (1828–1901) died on December 17th.

drawing and painting with prodigious skill. He was, in fact, one of the outstanding animal painters of more than his own time, and it is worth asking in what he fell short of genius?

In the monumental *Nettlefold Catalogue*,[3] C. Reginald Grundy suggested that 'over-specialized tuition' by Landseer's father, John Landseer the engraver, was partly to blame. He 'made little attempt either to give his son a good general education or to cultivate his taste for colour'. And as to Landseer's eventual fall from popular grace, Grundy's belief that 'Probably much unfavourable criticism has been inspired by the "catchy" titles' he too often affected, is cogent. Not the least part of Landseer's prodigious income was derived from engravings of his pictures, and it is partly with an eye on print-collectors that this chapter is written.

In days when a picture and its title were inseparable, the more 'catchy' the latter, the more it attracted the public. All the same, as Grundy points out, Landseer cannot be accused of painting a young buck and doe and calling it *The Honeymoon*, as this name – a 'seller' – was, with specious prettiness, inflicted on an engraving from an early work of his many years after his death. But for Landseer himself to have given the title of *None but the Brave deserve the Fair* to a conflict of stags was, in the long run at any rate, to risk a laugh in the wrong place. So, too, if more openly whimsical, *A Distinguished Member of the Royal Humane Society*, long accounted Landseer's 'best' picture of a dog, and even *There's Life in the Old Dog yet*, a cliff-rescue scene of considerable merit, were legends which, however initially acceptable, were in the end embarrassing. All these works belonged to 1838, a busy year for Landseer, and it is noticeable that, both before and after this phase, his titles were frequently less exuberant.

But the offending mood was also apparent in a certain lush sentimentality in some of the subjects themselves. At its best, Landseer's technique was immensely competent; so much so, perhaps, that he was the more easily able to trim his aesthetic sails to a masterful breeze.

5

That royal patronage, beneficial to Landseer the man, was in a measure detrimental to Landseer the artist, is a tragedy of good intentions. And if this seems to have been due less to the Queen's than to Prince Albert's influence, it still points the moral that artists should be true to themselves. The 'highly finished Germanic surface',[4] which now repels us in certain works of Landseer's and by no means in his alone, is, in more senses than one, a typically 'Victorian' symptom, bound up with exalted approval of smooth official portraits by Winterhalter – not that Frans-Xaver Winterhalter is a painter to be disdained.

So much of a 'Victorian' symptom was the highly finished manner that, when the blast of aesthetic impulse turned against it, many artists began to deprecate 'finish' in terms of downright dislike. It was (in an aesthetic sense) 'tight'. As will be seen later, there were sounder reasons than a dictate of fashion for this; but, as regards Landseer, one needs but contrast so

[3] C. Reginald Grundy: *A Catalogue of the Pictures and Drawings in the Collection of Frederick John Nettlefold* (Privately Issued, Vol. III, 1937).

[4] John Woodward: Introduction to Catalogue of *Paintings and Drawings by Sir Edwin Landseer*, RA (1961).

masterly a work as his dramatic portrait (at Burlington House) of the sculptor *John Gibson, RA* (1844 or 1850) with the so capable, commonplace, 'hard-as-nails' group of *Queen Victoria (and John Brown) at Osborne* (1866), in the Royal Collection, to appreciate what heights can be scaled, what opportunities missed, by an artist of outstanding capacity and, in the case of his *Gibson*, uninhibited judgment. Even so, one may quote a dictum attributed to Turner: 'If you only knew how difficult it is to paint even a decent picture, you would not say the severe things you do of those who *fail*.'[5]

6

Perhaps neither the *Gibson* nor the *Queen Victoria at Osborne* is what flashes on the screen of the mind when Landseer's name is invoked. As an animal painter, his skill, if not always his mood, is unchallengeable; but there is no harm in reminding a later generation that Landseer was not forever engaged on such subjects as *The Monarch of the Glen* (1851), which, originally intended for the Refreshment Room of the House of Lords, was obtusely turned down by the Commons on the score that 300 guineas was too high a price for it! So Landseer sold the picture to the Earl of Londesborough for 800 guineas, and the copyright to Henry Graves for a further 500 guineas. Since then, the picture's prices at auction have soared into thousands. Having passed through famous collections, it now belongs to John Dewar & Sons Ltd; and engravings of it were for long a staple of Victorian middle-class décor.

Not that Landseer was alone in the field of animal painting. Richard Ansdell, dismissed by C. H. Collins Baker in his *British Painting* (1933) as Landseer's 'chief follower and imitator', is a case in point; but no other 'Victorian' painter's reputation rose quite as high, or perhaps fell as low, as Landseer's. Not even Thomas Sidney Cooper, who became famous for his closely studied paintings of sheep and cattle, was religiously-minded, and nearly completed his century. H. G. Wells's ironic allusion to him in *The Invisible Man* (1897), when, in the siege of Dr Kemp's house, a revolver shot 'ripped a valuable Sidney Cooper', marks a stage in what was, then, a lessening appreciation of a well known painter.

Of 'Old' Herring and his brood, whose *œuvre* still poses an occasional problem to connoisseurs of such things, I say no more here than of others of the age whose reputation is secured by their adjacency to sporting art. But in the changed and more colourful phase of animal painting of the latter part of the nineteenth century, one should at least mention J. M. Swan whose period of training in Paris, under various of the most approved artists of the time, did much to re-vitalize rather stale pastures. Of Peter Graham, that indefatigable painter of Highland cattle, and who, born in 1836, lived on till 1921, it may be said that, for years and years, no Royal Academy Summer Exhibition would have been quite the same without him.

7

One must again beware of creating an impression that typically 'Victorian' painters were few in the land. There were, in fact, hundreds of them, great and small, famed or forgotten, and quite a few of them capable practitioners in their own field. The intense application with

[5] W. P. Frith: *My Autobiography and Reminiscences*, Chapter XI.

which the more typically High Victorian painters approached their themes, often of the life of the day, is well seen in such works as F. B. Barwell's slightly melodramatic *Adopting a Child* (1857), or, better-known, *The Last Day in the Old Home* (1862) which its painter, R. B. Martineau, crammed to the brim with scrupulously studied detail. A pupil of Holman Hunt, Martineau is said to have given ten years of his life to this prodigious performance: 'a novel in itself of life in the 'sixties', is William Gaunt's phrase for it.[6] Had one not seen Frith's *The Derby Day*, less a subject picture than a picture of subjects, one might feel even greater amazement at Martineau's laborious miracle.

Of Barwell, now again coming under notice, it remains to be said that, born in 1831, and having exhibited a considerable number of works at the Royal Academy and other London centres from 1858–87, he lived on till 1922 – in a world that had utterly changed.

8

Those two works, Barwell's and Martineau's, were both subject pictures of the 'literary' or 'anecdotal' type. So too were *The Derby Day* and a number of other works named or yet to be named in these pages. In its various manifestations, it was a type of art to which Victorians were greatly addicted. Not that 'subject' as such was of Victorian origin, since in one form or another, it had existed for more centuries than one cares to compute, and been practised by more highly accredited Masters than could be conveniently named. But so ripe was 'subject' in Victorian painting (and for many years afterwards) that eventually it became distasteful to persons unable, or unwilling, to distinguish sheep from goats.

In plain fact, there is nothing whatever wrong about subject painting, it is the nature of the subject, and, above all, how it is seen and *expressed* that count. The true gravamen of the anti-subject idea (eventually arising to sweep the board for a time) centred in the charge that thematic-content was overwhelming painterly qualities as such. Put otherwise: that artists were thinking too much of the theme and too little of the paint, and that a painter's true function was not that of an illustrator. For one reason or another, not always clearly defined, illustration was heresy.

That not a few painters did in fact fall into some such trap is undeniable; but where the 'advanced' of the day went adrift was in denying all merit to a picture *because* it had a perceptible or, if you will, literary content. One has only to look with an unjaundiced eye at the cream of Victorian (and Edwardian) subject pictures to see at a glance that their aesthetic balance was ably maintained. That the grand collapse (*pro tem.*) of the subject picture was post-Victorian does not affect the fact that it was heralded earlier, in the revolt against the already loosened bonds of Victorianism.

An important factor in the proliferation of Victorian subject painting of the more obviously 'literary' type – a good deal of it admirably done – centred in public taste. As Graham Reynolds has justly said:

'The Victorians were well read and loved to see illustrations of their favourite authors in the Academy; but the British genius is happily attuned to the practice of illustration, and

[6] William Gaunt: *The Pre-Raphaelite Tragedy* (1942).

Fig. 3. Propriety. Miss Propper, sitting for her portrait, is shocked by an artist taking off his coat on a hot day. Detail from a Fred Roe sequence in *Fun*. 15th September 1891.

the tradition in which Mulready, Frith and Leslie were working was at least as old as Hogarth'.[7]

It followed that, to satisfy their public, such performances had to be 'well done', and not 'daubs' – to employ a favourite synonym for artistic damnation.

All too often in art, the public gets what it deserves, and there can be no doubt but what public taste was ultimately responsible for much of the subject-picture explosion, and for tolerating the indifferent quality of those aspects of it which merely gave fodder to its foes. But this was not all. We glimpse a critical discrimination too often focused on mere correctitude – or what then passed as such.

9

Earlier and more commanding instances of critical 'big stick' could be given, but I may be excused for resurrecting a relatively late and forgotten example.

In 1888, a young artist began work on a portrait of his betrothed, seen posed in white, with a spray of scarlet blooms at her bosom, offsetting her dark, piled hair. Sincere, unforced, painterly, this canvas was placed in the next year's Royal Academy Summer Exhibition. What, of all responsible periodicals, had *The Athenæum* to say of it in June, 1889? I quote:

'Mr F. Roe's *Mabel* (1173), a comely damsel in a white evening dress, is decidedly spirited and agreeable, but the carnations are rough in touch, which they should not be in a lady's portrait. The charm of a youthful morbidezza and bright pure carnations suffers much from this. What can so tasteful an artist be thinking about thus to paint a lady's face.'

Which amounts to a reproof of ungentlemanly behaviour in painting. 'Carnation' is a good old word for the rosier flesh-tones, and the artist had had the temerity to allow brushwork to show in his rendering of 'a lady's face'. Plainly, in the view of the critic, this was 'not quite'.

[7] *Victorian Paintings*: Victoria and Albert Museum Small Picture Book, No. 10 (HMSO, 2nd ed., 1963).

10

At which point I find myself facing a digression on relative degrees of finish, of the use and abuse of handling, impasto, and kindred matters, better suited to a technical treatise. More important in our rummage of Victorian corners is to keep clearly in mind that there was not one long, placid harmony in the Victorian arts. Any conception of artists as a species of happy family, the lion lying down with the butterfly, the Leighton with the Whistler, is foredoomed to failure – and always will be so. To Academics, Pre-Raphaelitism was an outrage; to Pre-Raphaelites, Academism, in its various forms, was contemptible. Each side saw the other as preposterous, sterile, aesthetically damned. And when it came to Whistler – well there!

Yet all these and other trends of thought demanded a place in the Victorian arts, some of them far more significantly than, at the time, seemed credible. It was that same, scorpion-tongued 'Jimmy' Whistler who, among other notable services, did so much to set the pace for a simplified décor in our homes and exhibition galleries. Such changes took time to mature. From being regarded in opposing camps as dangerous revolutionaries, the Pre-Raphaelites now please in an oddly nostalgic way. Once so 'modern', now, to some eyes, so 'period', the Aesthetes waxed ridiculous by their own intensity. In W. E. Henley's facetious comment:

'I'm on for any Art that's 'Igh;
I talks as quite as I can splutter;
I keeps a Dado on the sly;
In fact, my form's the Bloomin' Utter!'

And when it came to 'the *bizarre*, French, "impressionist" style of painting recently imported into this country', Mr Frith could only warn of the 'incalculable damage' it would do 'to the modern school of English art'.[8] Yet, all the while, through revolution and counter-revolution, the Academics marched solidly on – or such is a superficial impression of what was, in truth, a phalanx of individualists. Academic art was not all-of-a-kind. It conformed to standards which themselves showed changes as years went by. Such changes did not influence everyone alike. Unless among the totally conventional, there is in art no marching 'shoulder to shoulder and blade by blade'. And, in the final analysis, it matters little whether an artist was Academic, Pre-Raphaelite, or what-have-you, even that alarming phenomenon an Impressionist (long reckoned a non-u word) so long as he or she is –. But let me resort to parable.

It was, I think, in his post-Victorian years that Sir Lawrence Alma-Tadema, one of the classical demi-gods of Victorian painting, was viewing a Royal Academy Summer Exhibition on Varnishing Day. With an artist-friend or two, the great man was appraising the exhibits, when he paused at one before which the group fell silent. Then spoke Alma-Tadema:

'That', said he, in effect, 'is by my friend Blank. He is a very good fellow. He is very careful. He paints very nicely; very nice pictures. But he is not an artist.'

And the group moved on . . .

11

That Alma-Tadema and other eminent Victorian classicists should have fallen as low as they did from their erstwhile Olympus is all-of-a-piece with the pattern of changing taste. Becom-

[8] Frith: *Autobiography*. (Quoted as an expression of academic thought of its time.)

ing vaguely bored with their former idols, the public, assimilating art-polemics, discovered that they did not like them after all. New and strange gods arose as the old ones faded away – until they, in their turn, should come again in a tempered glory.

It may be hard to make some readers believe that, in thus writing, I am not voicing my personal preferences; but one need not be a 'fan' of Alma-Tadema to allow him a very considerable level of achievement. Despite the classical splendours of his home in St John's Wood, and his orderly habit of numbering each *opus*, in Roman numerals, from i to ccccviii, his vision of ancient Greece, Rome, and Egypt, of Merovingian Gaul, was at times subtly seen through Victorian glasses, but to condemn such considerable works as *An Audience at Agrippa's* (1876) or the dramatic *Ave Cæsar! Io Saturnalia!* is merely short-sighted and prejudiced.

So, too, with Frederic, Lord Leighton, to give him the title he bore for so brief a span. That Leighton was probably the most dignified figure to grace the Presidential Chair of the Royal Academy – his very profile had a Jovian nobility – should not be forgotten. His presence was princely, and so, in a sense, was his art – even though, as William Gaunt reminds us in *Victorian Olympus* (1952), Queen Victoria 'did not entirely approve of Leighton's style of painting'. On the other hand, none less than Prince Albert himself had approved the purchase of *Cimabue's celebrated Madonna is carried in procession through the streets of Florence*, with which Leighton had made his début at the Royal Academy Exhibition (1855); so that was all right. But, if equally capable, Leighton's was a more masculine art than Alma-Tadema's, and his vision was greater, at its best monumental.

Yet neither Leighton, nor Alma-Tadema, nor others of their time painted flesh as William Etty had painted it. If Etty (1787–1849) does not more than edge into the Victorian Age, there is a Victorian or proto-Victorian mood about some of his work which demands his appearance on this little stage of mine. To put it bluntly, honest, unpretentious old Etty was one of the greatest painters of the nude the world has yet seen, and he needs no further glory.

Nothing could be further from the truth than the notion that Victorian taste completely eschewed the nude. In painting, sculpture, engraving, and ceramics, renderings of the nude might be, and often were, tempered by discretion, but were by no means unknown to possess a distinctly voluptuous quality; as, despite her decent sprinkling of transparent drapery, the healthily proportioned *Siren* painted (by T. J. Bott) on a Worcester porcelain plaque of 1883,[9] in a taste equivalent to that catered for by the C. F. Haviland factory at Limoges (Fig. 4).

That there were folk, artists as well as laymen, who viewed such qualities with horror, is also true. Prominent among them was J. C. Horsley,[10] whose abhorrence of the undraped model earned him the nickname of 'Clothes Horsley' from his fellows, and 'The Model "British Matron"' from a caricature in *Punch* by that brilliant cartoonist Linley Sambourne.

Horsley's house, part butting onto the pavement, is yet a familiar landmark in Kensington Church Street. One wonders what would have been the old Royal Academician's comment,

[9] Geoffrey Bemrose: *Nineteenth Century English Pottery and Porcelain* (Faber, 1952), pl. 72.

[10] He who had designed the 'first' Christmas Card for [Sir] Henry Cole in 1843.

Fig. 4. Limoges Porcelain wall-plaque (C. F. Haviland factory) dated 1886 (11 in. diam.); and (R) an aesthetic ('Bamboo') 'Ironstone China' Plate by J. Meir & Son, Tunstall, Staffs. (*Mr Winslow Rhode*)

had he known that, in years as yet unborn, another R.A., Sir William Russell Flint, would be painting – and admirably painting – a whole galaxy of nudes in nearby Peel Street? But these have no bearing on Victorian art.

12

At the risk of neglecting such other important fields as those of portraiture, landscape and marine, sporting, and what that fine old documentarist 'Algie' Graves classified as 'domestic' subjects, let us glance at the variations, within academic art, of historical and costume painting.

Time was when 'historical painter' was a status symbol of quality. It indicated a superior branch of painting, inspired by lofty ideals – or such was an idea inherited from the Georgian past. Ruskin was not first in demanding lofty inspiration, nobly expressed.

In practice, and with echoes of the Grand School to colour it, this resulted not alone in ennobling themes, but in immense canvases: as though there were an essential link between bulk and nobility. There is more than whimsy in Thackeray's ironical description of 'George Rumbold's' picture of *Alfred in the Neatherd's Cottage* (72 × 48 ft.), in which 'the mere muffin, of which the outcast king is spoiling the baking, is two feet three in diameter'.[11] Many very large pictures were actually painted, though a number of them have since been cut up, or

[11] Thackeray: *Our Street* (1848).

Fig. 5. Admiring a Maclise in the 1850s. From Cuthbert Bede's *The Adventures of Mr Verdant Green.* (Part III, 1853)

completely destroyed. And, if less gigantic, it was quite usual to send six-footers to the Academy, though the claims of smaller, including what were known as cabinet, pictures were, of course, also allowed. To this day, Gallery IX at Burlington House is called the 'Gem Room' by those with long memories.

13

'"Do you see that picture?" asked Miss Patty; and she directed Verdant's attention to a small but exquisite oil-painting by Maclise. It was in illustration of one of Moore's melodies, "Come rest in this bosom, my own stricken deer!" The lover had fallen upon one knee at his mistress's feet, and was locked in her embrace. With a look of fondest love she had pillowed his head upon her bosom. . . .'

And so forth. Though I yield to few in my liking for *The Adventures of Mr Verdant Green,*[12] it was not until this present book was in prospect that it occurred to me to check that fulsome passage.

Daniel Maclise *had* painted such a picture, which he sent under that slightly embarrassing 'Come rest in this bosom' title, to the 1847 Academy, and 'Cuthbert Bede's' illustration shows just how that kind of subject looked in a domestic setting of its time. It is not my intention to draw any fine distinction between 'historical' and 'historical costume painting',

[12] 'Cuthbert Bede, BA' (Rev. Edward Bradley): *The Adventures of Mr Verdant Green, An Oxford Freshman* (1853–56).

if, indeed, any practical difference exists. Artists who painted the one, glided easily into painting the other. Maclise's canvas of *The Play Scene in Hamlet* (R.A., 1842) is, within its own convention, a rich and not unimpressive example of Otrantoesque Gothick. One feels that the grim guards in the background, in their effective if unsuitable harnesses, are alone worth the money.

In his *Autobiography*, Frith tells of his own early adoration of Maclise ('Of course, I copied his faults'); and of another young artist who told him: '"Maclise is out and away the greatest artist that ever lived."' The like has been said of other painters, not all of whom have stayed the course; though Maclise's merits were not negligible, and his line profiles of celebrated contemporaries are valuable documents. Nor can the costume paintings by William Mulready, C. R. Leslie, E. M. Ward, or Frith himself be lightly dismissed. In some, at least, the performance is impressive, and a clear attempt has been made to break away from the garb of melodrama in favour of dress truer to the periods involved.

14

To what extent considerations of accuracy should prevail in a work of art, as distinct from a scientific reconstruction, depends very much on cases. My father, himself a painter who gave a good deal of thought to his 'costume' details, and whose *Aristocrats*, 1790, was to be that phenomenon the 'picture of the year' at the R.A. (1910), held 'that the cut of a coat should never be allowed to intrude or assert itself on a canvas to the detriment of the rendering of a scene, as a whole . . .'.[13] This means that the picture comes first, and that there is a distinction between accuracy and a suggestion of accuracy. Indeed, it could be argued that, within the limitations of their knowledge of the past, some of the earlier Victorian costume painters were almost pedantic. Frith's *Honeywood introducing the Bailiffs to Miss Richland and his Friends* (1850), in the Victoria and Albert Museum, is an effective example of the union of a vast amount of detail and characterization in a literally polished performance. But a deterioration 'into that glassy smoothness of which E. M. Ward' was, in Collins Baker's view,[14] 'the best exponent', was doomed to become hidebound, lingering on long after it had ceased to be in the least modish.

Such crowded compositions as E. M. Ward's *Doctor Johnson in the ante-room of Lord Chesterfield, waiting for an audience, 1748*, (1845), or *The South-Sea Bubble* (1847), were illustrations which anyone who had heard of Dr Johnson, Lord Chesterfield, or the South-Sea Bubble could examine at leisure with interest and even instruction. They were, too, remarkably well done in their way, with nothing of the 'daub' about them. But, as the nineteenth century progressed, influences arose which put these and works of a like kidney in the shade. Nor were these influences such as derived from the Pre-Raphaelites, or from Burne-Jones who, in appropriate moments, not only painted armour and costume, but invented such trappings to suit his Arthurian dreamland. Artists and students were studying the more virile Dutch masters, Rembrandt and Hals, with a new eye; Whistler was discovering that

[13] Quoted by 'Austin Chester' [Mrs Savage]: *The Art of Mr Fred Roe* (*Windsor Magazine*, March, 1908).

[14] C. H. Collins Baker: *British Painting* (1933).

power-house of energy controlled reposing in the mighty achievement of Velazquez. The hour had struck for a change in the manner of costume painting, and not in that only.

Thus, while a dwindling allegiance was maintained to the meticulous style of the past, new men arose who, without sacrificing subject-interest, accepted brushwork and handling as in themselves expressive and stimulating. This did not necessarily involve any great freedom of attack, though in some hands it did so. But the idea of surface-finish as an artistic perfection in itself was ceasing to attract; and if a painter saw an advantage in spanking on a high light with a dextrous flick of the brush, or in the loosening process technically known as 'knocking the picture about', he zestfully did so. 'Crumby' paint began to come back. It had been good enough for Rembrandt that consummate master (himself a costume painter, when he so chose). And what, in some moods of Sir Sploshua?

Seeing that some of the newer generation of costume painters could look back to the 1840s or '50s, there is no wonder that not all of them equally reacted to such influences as these. One may instance S. E. Waller whose smoothly stated costume pieces in architectural settings (*The Empty Saddle*, *The Day of Reckoning*, etc.) had their lease of popularity. Charles Green, now chiefly remembered for his illustrations to Dickens's *Christmas Books*, as republished by *Pears's Annual* in the 1890s, can be seen as a robust development of sheer Englishness, reputed, in his own day, to command three-figure sums for his elaborately detailed water-colours. On the other hand, John Seymour Lucas, nephew of John Lucas, a once fashionable portraitist, was greatly attracted to Van Dyck, his outlook being later broadened by a study of the freer Dutch masters. Moreover, like Whistler, he 'discovered' Velazquez though, unlike Whistler, he was able to visit the Prado.

This, his first trip to Spain, in 1881,[15] was made in the company of Andrew Carrick Gow, also a costume painter, and Sydney Williams Lee, one of Lucas's pupils who, though by profession an architect, exhibited a number of pictures at Burlington House. 'I remember when I was in Spain with Seymour Lucas and Andrew Gow, the Royal Academicians, . . .'

15

Seymour Lucas's art was accomplished; he was a draughtsman, a colourist, a handler of paint, with an eye for a good composition. If at times smacking of the studio, his scenes of the past have an air of actuality. The studio[16] at his London home, the Shakespeareanly-named New Place in Woodchurch Road, West Hampstead, had the air of the hall of an old country mansion, panelled and garnished with arms and armours and old oak furniture. It even possessed a glazed-in minstrels' gallery, which served as a models' changing room, a glory-hole, and (as was rumoured) a point of vantage whence meetings of the Kernoozers' Club could be unofficially monitored. Indeed, one of the significant points about not only Lucas but Charles Green and various other of the better-known costume painters of the time, was

[15] Lucas's second trip to Spain in 1891, made in connexion with his picture *1588: News of the Spanish Armada* (R.A., 1893), involved him in the railway crash at Burgos, when his travelling companions (not those of 1881) were killed, and he sustained a fractured leg which left him limping for life.

[16] More precisely Lucas's studio; Mrs Seymour Lucas had her own studio upstairs.

that their work and their lives seemed centred in a not very clearly defined projection from the historical past, plus such more or less up-to-date amenities as might be called for.[17]

Not that this meant a withdrawal from the world. Besides being a considerable painter and, in due course, a member of the Royal Academy, 'Semolicus' was a notable antiquary, FSA, a leading light in the old Kernoozers' Club and, later, of the (still surviving) Meyrick Society which last, under its original title of the Junior Kernoozers' Club, was founded in 1890. Both these exclusive bodies began as studio societies meeting at members' homes for the informal and expert discussion of arms, armours, and antiquarian matters. Their influence was considerable. Indeed, the part played by nineteenth-century artists (other than Morris) and their friends in the appreciation and preservation of antiquities, has yet to be fully acknowledged.

Moreover, most figure painters kept a wardrobe of miscellaneous costume and accessories, Charles Green, Lucas and his friend Ernest Crofts, Edwin A. Abbey, Talbot Hughes, Sir James Linton, James Prinsep Beadle a well-known painter of military subjects (for whom, in a much later year, I was to pose for part of Napoleon Bonaparte, and whose Boer War picture *The Empty Saddle* was entirely distinct from Waller's earlier costume subject of similar title), are a few of the names that leap like fish in the pool of one's memory. Indeed some of these wardrobes were of such fine importance as to warrant their preservation. The arrays of antique costume formed by Lucas and Abbey, including many rare items, were acquired for the London Museum; Talbot Hughes's assemblage swelled the relevant section at the Victoria and Albert Museum.

16

Not that Lucas's costume painting and Abbey's had anything else in common. Lucas's was the more matter-of-fact; where he composed, Abbey *designed*. Abbey's *Richard, Duke of Gloucester, and the Lady Anne* (1896) was more than a medieval subject; it was seen with a medieval eye. And in a small painting of the *Murder of Henry VI*, Abbey anticipated film technique by taking what would have been later known as a high-angle shot – down on the body of the king. It was very effective as was Abbey's rendering of the Tent Scene in *Julius Cæsar:* the ghost's imperial robe patterned with gouts of blood. Such imaginative flights had no place in Lucas's *œuvre*; which is not to say that 'Semolicus' was lacking in ideas. Far from it. He was a painter of the picturesque, with a strong sense of realism; who thought more of Gainsborough than of Reynolds, and who advised at least one of his pupils to have a good look at Wilkie's *Blind Man's Buff* in the National Gallery.

17

As a hitherto unpublished item of documentary interest, the instrument by which Fred Roe became a pupil of Seymour Lucas is worth placing on record.[18] The whole process smacked

[17] See also Roe: *Victorian Furniture* (1952), Chapter 15.

[18] So far as I know Seymour Lucas (RA) never himself hyphenated his name, though his elder and surviving son Sidney Charles Seymour-Lucas (1878–1954), also an accomplished painter, did so. Seymour Lucas, RA, was so named after his mother, Mrs Henry Lucas, formerly Elizabeth Seymour.

3. One of Sir Edwin Landseer's noblest paintings: JOHN GIBSON, RA, sculptor of the famous 'Tinted Venus'. *By permission of Royal Academy of Arts, London*

4. Seymour Lucas's *A 'Whip' for Van Tromp: The Admiralty, 1652*, one of the features of the 1883 R.A. Exhibition, with (R) Rutland Barrington posing as the Earl of Sandwich (fingering moustache). Owned by the artist, the seventeenth-century oak table now belongs to Mrs Michael Maynard. (*Leicester Museum and Art Gallery*)

5. *Pepys encounters Nell Gwyn in Drury Lane*. Project in quill pen and sepia ink, by Fred Roe, dated 22.4. [18]95. (*Author*)

6. As it was in his heyday: Seymour Lucas's studio at New Place, Woodchurch Road, West Hampstead. (*Photo. Walter Withall*)

Victorian elegance—and a tense moment in the gloaming. Illustration by Fred. Walker, ARA, for Dutton Cook's *The Prodigal Son* in *Once a Week* (1862)

of tradition. In 1884, Roe, then a student at Heatherley's, was greatly impressed by Lucas's *After Culloden: Rebel Hunting* in that year's Academy, where it was 'bought by the Chantrey'. Lucas was approached, and, after seeing specimens of the young man's work, accepted him as a pupil subject to a legal Agreement between the parties. This document (one copy of which is in my possession) was completed on April 28, 1885, and contained four provisions. Summarized, these were: (1) In consideration of the sum of £400, Lucas will 'teach and instruct' Roe

'in the Profession Art or Calling of an Artist or Painter in Oil Colours as now exercised by the said John Seymour Lucas and for such purpose will devote so much time as may be necessary on two days a week between the hours of 10 and 5 o'clock at "New Place". . . . for the period of two years from the date hereof',

Lucas to provide luncheon on the said days; Roe

'to provide all materials and models at his own cost also the required costumes provided that he shall be entitled to make use of any costume belonging to the said John Seymour Lucas which may be at "New Place" aforesaid'.

Breathlessly turning to Clause Two, we find an arrangement for payment of the premium by instalments, with normal safeguards; and in Clause Three – 'It is also agreed . . . . that the instruction to be given . . . . shall be confined to general supervision and advice, so as not to interfere with' Lucas 'working at his own pictures'. (Thus, the instruction was not elementary but advanced, the young student being already a proficient draughtsman; though Lucas advised him to take evening classes at the St Martin's School of Art, where he himself once studied, for the sake of average practice.) Finally, Clause Four of the Agreement provided that, in the event of any dispute arising between the parties, John Pettie, RA (that distinguished costume painter) was named as referee.

It is doubtful whether many such documents, as between one artist and another, have survived from the Victorian past. To round off the story, be it added that the signatures of the contracting parties were witnessed by the same Sydney Williams Lee who figured in the Madrid expedition of 1881. It was he who designed Lucas's studio at New Place; and the Mabel (whose portrait was not altogether approved by the *Athenæum's* critic) was Lee's elder daughter. She and Fred Roe were married at Putney in 1890.

18

One sure test of the general interest in subject painting in Victorian (and Edwardian) times is the way in which pictures impressed themselves on the public memory. Millais's *The Boyhood of Raleigh* (1870) and Lucas's *The Armada in Sight* (1880) are cases in point. Neither is by any means its creator's best work, yet, thanks in part to engravings and reproductions, both have shown a survival value so far denied to finer aesthetic achievements by the same men. Having thus been grafted on the public consciousness, these compositions retain a

Fig 6. At a Garden Party in 1899: The Author's Mother in silhouette.

measure of their grip on it. They remain fodder for cartoonists or the illustrators of pictorial crossword puzzles. Clearly Lucas's conception of Drake, 'wood' in hand, has become that of the man-in-the-street, whether or not the man-in-the-street is aware of it. But who would not sacrifice the studied arrangement of *The Armada in Sight* for the admirably nimble brushwork of that jolly little 'Lucas' *The Nimble Galliard* (1901); or, for all its majestic design, *The Boyhood of Raleigh* for that exquisitely sensitive poem in paint, created before Millais had quitted Pre-Raphaelitism, *The Little Blind Girl* (1856), described by Rossetti as 'one of the most touching and perfect things I know'.

A noticeable feature of all these works is the complete aptness of their titles. It is not, I think, untrue to suggest that, as the nineteenth century progressed, increasing attention was paid to the titles of pictures. From being merely descriptive, they acquired an arresting character, completely integrated with the work itself; and whether or not the title suggested the picture or the picture the title is of little importance.

Admittedly, Turner could give us a *Rain, Steam and Speed: The Great Western Railway* (1844); but then Turner was Turner, and the picture became everywhere known by its shortened title. Millais's *Chill October* (1870); John Brett's seascape, *Britannia's Realm* (1880); Frank Bramley's *A Hopeless Dawn* (1882); Lucas's *A 'Whip' for Van Tromp – The Admiralty, 1652* (1883) (in which the celebrated singer Rutland Barrington posed for the figure of the first Earl of Sandwich); Roe's *The Traitor's Wife* (1895), painted before his post-Lucasian development; and Harry Adams's discerning snow-scene *Winter's Sleep* (1900) are representative of the kind of dramatically effective and wholly integrated titles encountered.

Nor was the aesthetic the sole point to be reckoned with. There were practical advantages. A good subject deserved a good title, and a good, catchy title could do more than sell a picture;

it could make hay for the artist in the matter of selling the copyright. It could, and did, happen that an artist might do better from the disposal of copyrights, or sundry reproduction rights in a work, than by the sale of the picture itself. Similarly, the quotation, usually from an accredited author or poet, which might follow the title, had the side effect of making a break in a closely-printed catalogue.

Nevertheless, the idea that a picture and its title were indissolubly one was accepted as a matter of course. Granted that a good title could be, and too often was, an excuse for a bad picture, there is no reason why a good picture should bear a scamped title, if its creator had the wit to invent it.

Ravel saw no bar to composing a *Pavanne for a Dead Infanta.*

19

For a reason which will emerge, I have reserved one of the most notable cases of titling: Frederick Walker's remarkable water-colour of *The Three Fates*, which he sent to the Old Society in 1868. In that it was based on one of Walker's own black-and-white illustrations to Miss Thackeray's (later Lady Ritchie's) *Jack the Giant Killer*, this was about as 'literary' a painting as well could be. But in Walker's hands it acquired a life of its own. His presentation of the Fates as three elderly Victorian ladies – one grimly watchful, one smiling, one in mourning, erect and gaunt, cutting a thread from a workbasket as a young woman springs from her chair in that so prim Victorian sitting-room – gains in subjective horror from the very commonplaceness of its setting. It grows on one that here is one of the subtly terrifying pictures in Victorian art: a terror which only a poet in paint – and Frederick Walker was called 'The Tennyson of Painting' – could achieve without sensationalism. Something of the same tension is evident in a lesser-known illustration of his, for Dutton Cook's *The Prodigal Son*, in *Once a Week*, 1862.

Frederick Walker (the 'Little Billee' of Du Maurier's *Trilby*) had a first cousin whose son Leonard Walker was a family friend of ours. Born in 1877, he lived on till 1964, having become one of the most significant stained-glass artists of his time, and whose personal form of Impressionism in water-colour is strangely moving.

It was in his late age that, one afternoon, I was talking to Leonard Walker in his studio near Swiss Cottage. We had got on to the subject of Walker, and I spoke of *The Three Fates.*

Said Leonard Walker to me: 'The couch he used in it is under there', waving a long bony hand at a trestle-table loaded with books and drawings.

Sure enough, there, in the shadow beneath, was the very sofa, smaller than Walker had made it look in *The Three Fates*, and by now dusty and tattered – but the self-same sofa. It was a memorable moment.

20

In a sense, *The Three Fates* was a forerunner of that far from unmixed blessing the Problem Picture: a sizeable part of whose attraction was in the questions it posed to viewers. What did it mean ? What will happen ? Is she guilty ? Will he forgive her ? If the main vogue for problem

Fig. 7. *'Have You Caught It?'* Gordon Thomson's caricature of W. F. Yeames's *Prince Arthur and Hubert*, from *Fun's Academy Skits.*

pictures belongs to the next reign, the most enduringly renowned (or notorious) painting of this kind was Victorian. W. F. Yeames's *When did you last see your father?* (1878) has become a byword. (But it was Yeames who was capable of so distinguished a composition as the *Prince Arthur and Hubert* (1882), at Manchester.) Had more problem pictures been possessed of a higher proportion of painterly qualities, their significance might have been greater; but a point not always taken is that such works, often competently done, were, in their noontide of popularity, as much disliked by subject painters in other fields as they were by the critical faculty. Both sides, for once united in disapproval, viewed the tendency as a menace to art.

As much a menace, in its own way, had become that quintessence of the sugary aspects of Victorianism (and Edwardianism), the 'chocolate box'. The pity of it is that the Hon. John Collier, who became (despite his disclaimer) the principal prophet of the problem picture, was capable of higher things, among them the impressive portrait of *Darwin*, old and cloaked, of which there is a signed replica (1883) in London's National Portrait Gallery. It is well worth anyone's notice.

21

At which stage, my imagination projects an image of a puzzled, and slightly contemptuous, art lover disposed to impugn both my taste and my logic. Have you no more to say about Whistler and nothing to say, good or bad, about Sargent? You bring in Frederick Walker, but omit his admirable friend and contemporary G. J. Pinwell. If you name kindly J. P. Beadle in military painting, why not also W. B. Wollen or R. Caton Woodville, the latter living next door to Beadle in Eldon Road, Kensington, and, among much else, illustrator of Stanley Weyman's *Under the Red Robe* (1894)? Or, so famed in their day, Robert Gibb for *The Thin Red Line, October 25, 1854* (1882); Elizabeth Thompson (Lady Butler), for *The Roll Call* (1874) with which she bounded into fame at the age of twenty-seven, the moving if contrived composition of *The Remnants of an Army* (1879), and the vigorous, thundering charge of the Greys in *Scotland for Ever!* (1881).

I plead guilty, but do not retract. What can I say about Whistler or Sargent that has not been said a hundred times? Whistler was a great, exploratory artist; Sargent a great adept in technical attack. Both demonstrate the principle of up-and-down popularity; for, even in their own day, opinion on their merits was sharply divided. I am looking at a letter of as late as 1912 in which an elderly gentleman, far from devoid of artistic sense, described his visit to the R.A. Summer Exhibition that year. 'I think Mr Sargent's pictures must be meant for a joke, I cannot take them seriously.'

Again, what new can I say about the progression of landscape painters from John Sell Cotman, high master of economical statement, to B. W. Leader who began life as Benjamin Williams, and who saw every leaf on the tree with such patient fidelity. On David Cox, that beloved landscape painter, I have written two books already, and dare not write a third; whereas the ever-voluble George C. Haité, brilliant colourist, impressionist, and designer of everything from textiles and wall-papers to the original cover of *The Strand Magazine* would demand a book to himself. But I would not omit all mention of Thomas Shotter Boys, master of cityscapes; nor of Dickens's friend, Clarkson Stanfield, that gifted master of marines; nor of our old friend Edwin Hayes, whose *Sunset at Sea: from Harlyn Bay, Cornwall*, was 'kicked out' of the R.A., only to be honourably placed, and bought by the Chantrey in a later year (1894). And in the more typically 'period' field, what of Edwin Long, whose *Babylonian Marriage Market* (1875) was thought such high art in its day? Or what, again, of those regular exhibition features, 'Joe' Farquharson's snowscapes which Harry Graham was at a later time to crystallize in a couplet speaking of:

> 'Farquharson's eternal snow,
> And Swan's eternal leopards.'[19]

But Swan, if not his 'eternal leopards' (or lions or tigers or panthers), has already been mentioned.

Then, too, both residing – residing is the word – in Melbury Road, Kensington, with old, apocalyptic G. F. Watts a few doors away in Little Holland House, were the last original illustrators of Dickens in the novelist's own lifetime: Marcus Stone, with his long curling moustachios, love of cats, and (maybe) a deeper belief in the validity of his own pictorial romaunts than is always allowed him; and Sir Luke Fildes, neatly bearded, precise of speech, who had taken such vast pains over that able subject picture of his, *The Doctor* (1891). To obtain the desired effect, he had a small cottage-room run up within his tall studio at Woodlands House, and posed his models within it, in a convincing cross-lighting.

[19] Harry Graham: *The Royal Academy* (in the *Observer*, May 11, 1913).

And, moving across to Portland Place, one found the pillared drawing-room seen in a number of Sir W. Q. Orchardson's pictures. Orchardson's thinnish paint may seem frail at times, though the flashing brushwork of which he was capable, as in the table appointments of *The Young Duke* (1889), can be little short of miraculous. If his *Napoleon on board the Bellerophon* (1880) is for some hackneyed, its exquisite sentiment survives; though it is in one of Orchardson's scenes of contemporary life, *Her Mother's Voice* (1888) – another of those integrated titles – that one sees, as through a window, into a well-off late Victorian home. 'Orchardson's art and his paint are two distinct things' is a comment to me by a brother-brush of his who admired him. It bears thinking about.

No, I do not apologize. This book is called *Victorian Corners*: it is one long digression, and we shall yet meet Victorian artists in some of them. Yet, come to think of it, nothing has been said of not only one of the memorable 'Victorian' painters, but one of the most fascinating recorders of the Victorian scene. His name was J. J. J. Tissot, and he was French – with a tragic romance in St John's Wood.

THREE

From Plain to Fussy, and Back

'Gone were the Morris papers and gone the severe cretonnes, gone were the Arundel prints that had adorned the walls of her drawing-room in Ashley Gardens.'
W. SOMERSET MAUGHAM

I

PREMISING that the title of this chapter is as makeshift as are most generalizations, it nonetheless gives a quick view of trends in Victorian taste. But we are still faced by a like problem – What *is* Victorian painting; what *is* Victorian furniture? There is no supposing that 'Early Victorian' sprang spontaneously into being in 1837, like Athene from the brain of Zeus, when the young Queen was proclaimed.

When that happened, quite a variety of furniture styles were in use, their up-to-dateness or otherwise being partly dependent on their owners' means and modishness, partly on whether or not they saw any point in preferring what was then 'modern' to familiar, established ideas, or simply because old friends are best and anyway they couldn't afford it.

Thus, a smart 'town' interior was still decked out in the best kind of 'Regency' and its immediate aftermath (which I see no cause to call 'Adelaide' furniture). Homes of less smartness might well retain 'Georgian' furniture (not forgetting the freely named 'Chippendale', 'Hepplewhite', 'Sheraton', and 'Adam'), and so back to the earlier Georges and Queen Anne; indeed, here and there, earlier still. And if such furniture was deemed too dowdy for the salon, or the Colonel's study where he slept after nuncheon, it might be well enough for upstairs rooms or the servants' quarters. Naturally, a good deal depended on other considerations than those of taste or depth of pocket, and any conception of all town houses as being necessarily *à la mode*, whereas all country houses were 'very otherwise', is plainly false. For our purpose, it suffices to start the ball rolling with 'Regency'.

Now, Regency furniture was not all of a kind. Some of it was ornate and exotic; but, on the whole, it was the plainer varieties which filtered down into good, solid, run-of-the-mill Victorianism. Even so, the rather odd Gothic which had inspired Walpole and Chatterton was not dead, and, under the influence of Walter Scott (among others), took a new direction.

This resulted in what later became known as 'Abbotsford' furniture, on which I have written elsewhere.[20] So far as I know, the limits of Abbotsford furniture or the age of the 'label' itself have not been decided. The latter was certainly in use by 1901 without an explanatory gloss, which suggests that it was already in (a mainly pejorative) currency. That it has been freely applied, thus mopping up other styles, seems probable; but the problem is one more suited to an authority on terminology, such as John Gloag. Though other articles are at times rather vaguely involved, its application to tall-back chairs, the *older* of them dating

[20] *Victorian Furniture* (Phoenix House Ltd, 1952); *Home Furnishing with Antiques* (John Baker, 1965).

Fig. 8. Quilp and Tom Scott (L) use Abbotsford chairs in this wood-engraving by C. Gray after Phiz, in Dickens's *Old Curiosity Shop* (1840-1).

from somewhere about the 1830s – 50s or 60s, is safe enough, though remnants of the style are recognizable much later. That such items, often based on latish seventeenth-century design, were at one time erroneously thought to reflect anything onwards from 'Elizabethan' or even earlier taste, has long since ceased to mislead collectors. Though Abbotsford chairs (or many of them) were often overloaded with turnings and curlicues, relatively simple and attractive examples, usually of lighter dimensions, have survived; and more massive, ultra-Gothic fantasies are – or were – not wanting (*cp.* Fig. 8).

Abbotsforditis existed side-by-side with simpler styles, and became a diminishing habit, unless we drag in 'baronial' tables, sideboards, bookcases, and other large items, of which the prevailing characteristics are mainly those of the 'bulgeydingo' period. But to call 'Abbotsford' all retrospectively-designed items is clearly *ultra vires*, as witness the curious case of a 'Gothic' chair at Hughenden Manor House, sometime country seat of Benjamin Disraeli.

2

'It is all done, you are the Lady of Hughenden', wrote Disraeli to his wife in 1848. The old manor house was theirs, and they loved it. The comely if Gothicized building remained with their kindred till 1937. It now belongs to the National Trust and is a Disraeli museum with an agreeably un-museumlike atmosphere, as though the great statesman had just flung down the pen, where one sees it lying on the Study writing-table.

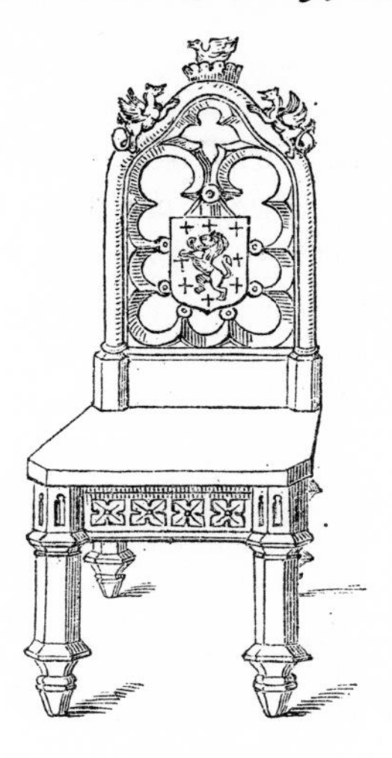

Fig. 9. A Gothic Hall Chair, designed by Edward Buckton Lamb (1806–69). From Loudon's *Encyclopedia* (1833)

But it is a chair in the Entrance Hall with which we are concerned: item 3 in the official guide to *Hughenden Manor* (Country Life Ltd, for the National Trust, 1965), which lists it as 'THE ABBOT OF MEDMENHAM'S CHAIR', followed by a brief note on the notorious Hell Fire Club, and ending: 'The Abbot's Chair, it is to be presumed, came from West Wycombe.'

In this corner of Buckinghamshire, any relic of the Hell Fire Club is very much at home. Modern attempts to whitewash that dubious brotherhood have failed to dispel its nasty reputation. With that we have no business, all that here matters being that the self-styled 'monks' of Medmenham Abbey and West Wycombe, otherwise the Hell Fire Club, were a typically eighteenth-century concept, whereas, in my opinion, the 'Abbot's Chair' at Hughenden, so far from being eighteenth-century, is a stoutly built and elaborately carved piece in the Gothic taste of the mid-nineteenth. Furthermore, it is utterly unlike the furnishings of West Wycombe Church, as re-edified and re-equipped 'in the Grecian gusto' by Sir Francis Dashwood in 1763 – the year in which he became Lord le Despencer.

Nor is that all. The Hughenden chair displays on its back a shield of arms which, when I saw it, had none of the air of an addition to the structure. This shield is carved in relief with the arms of *Disraeli* impaling *Viney*.[21] What, it may be asked, are the Disraeli arms doing on the back of a Dashwood chair; arms, moreover, displaying an impalement meaningless before Benjamin Disraeli's marriage in 1839?

Even so, is the chair necessarily as old as 1839? To my eye, it savoured more of the Gothic Revivalism of the 1860s or thereabouts; at which point one reminds oneself that Edward Buckton Lamb, the architect who gothicized Hughenden for the future Viscountess Beaconsfield in 1862–3, is known to have designed chairs in the Gothic taste. Has this a bearing on the

[21] Fully tinctured, the arms on the chair-back would be: *Per saltire gules and argent, a triple-towered castle* (*or 'tower of Castile'*) *in chief argent, with 2 lions rampant in fess sable, and in base a spreadeagle or* (Disraeli), impaling *Argent, a bunch of grapes, stalked and leaved proper* (Viney). Actually, Mrs Disraeli was born Evans, but her mother's brother was Major-General Sir James Viney, KCH, whose eventual heiress Mrs Disraeli became.

true history of the Hughenden chair? Or was there *another* chair veritably used by the pseudo-abbot, the tradition of which was somehow confused with that of the seat now at Hughenden?

Plaisted's brief mention of the chair, in his *Manor and Parish Records of Medmenham* (1925), implies without asserting that it was one of the relics shown to visitors to Medmenham towards the close of the eighteenth century; but that, I submit is impossible. My suggestion is that if the Disraelis in fact acquired a Hell Fire Club chair, it was not this one.

Or is it too wild a guess that the idea could have sprung from a deadpan Disraelian quip which, by force of repetition, was taken more seriously than its illustrious creator had ever intended?

3

Meanwhile, the relative plainness of Early Victorian furniture was mainly an outcrop from earlier styles, and this plainness was holding its own. Ornament there was, of a kind relevant to the mostly solid-type furniture on which it appeared. There are masses of chairs in mahogany or rosewood, or of some disguised lesser wood: chairs which, minor details apart, carried a modified Regency tradition till late in the century. Based on a classical type, the kind of chair sometimes called 'Tablet-top', its chief characteristic a deep back-rail with or

Fig. 10. At the 'Mitre', showing a 'Tablet-top' chair (L) From *The Adventures of Mr Verdant Green, An Oxford Freshman* by 'Cuthbert Bede'. (Part I, 1851)

without a lesser rail below it, was, in its various forms, remarkably persistent. Even more typically Victorian, though the type was emerging a little earlier than the reign itself, was the 'Balloon-back': a generic name for chairs with 'waisted' backs swelling to a pronounced loop. There were numerous variations of this popular type, some distinguished by names of their own, 'Double-C', 'Rise-and-drop', and 'Buckle-back' among them.[22] And all the while the homely Windsor, which John Gloag has so justly called 'the triumphant survivor of the native English tradition of chair design',[23] and to which I once devoted an entire book, was being, is still being, made and will (one hopes) maintain its long trek down the centuries.

[22] John Gloag, FSA, HON. ARIBA: *The Englishman's Chair* (George Allen & Unwin, 1964); F. Gordon Roe: *Victorian Furniture* (Phoenix House Ltd, 1952).

[23] Gloag: *op. cit.*

Fig. 11. Typical 'Rise-and-drop Balloon-back' chairs in an illustration by Fred. Walker, ARA, for Thomas Speight's *Tenants at Number Twenty-Seven* in *Once a Week* (1860).

4

One little byway which calls for passing mention concerns tea-caddies made in the form of miniature sideboards. Without our going deeply into what was, after all, a minor vagary of fashion, there seems to have been something of a taste for such things about the second quarter of the nineteenth century: at any rate, some of those I have seen were roughly datable as such. Two good examples were shown in the Exhibition of Queen Mary's Art Treasures at the Victoria and Albert Museum; a plainer one, in my possession, is illustrated here.

This latter lacks, and has never had, the low back-board often found on this type of pedestal sideboard – as, for instance, the 'handsome but rather expensive sideboard' here reproduced from Loudon's *Encyclopædia* (1833). Comments Loudon: 'The expense may, however, be reduced without materially injuring the effect, by omitting the carved foliage attached to the drawers.' Though simpler in design, the caddy is clearly related to this build of sideboard. It stands $5\frac{3}{4}$ in. high, and is $11\frac{3}{4}$ in. long. Access to the interior is by lifting the top, which is hinged at the back and can be locked through a keyhole on the underside of the superstructure. The pedestals, which would be doored in a real sideboard, are hollow, each with its ivory-knobbed lid.

Here, in small, is the kind of thing Early Victorians would have deemed an essential part of any civilized dining-room.

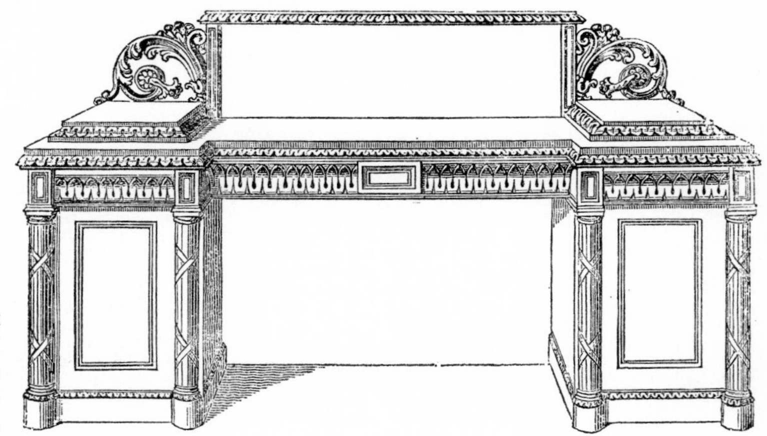

Fig. 12. 'A handsome but rather expensive sideboard,' allowing for a mirror-panel in the back board. From J. C. Loudon's *Encyclopædia* (1833).

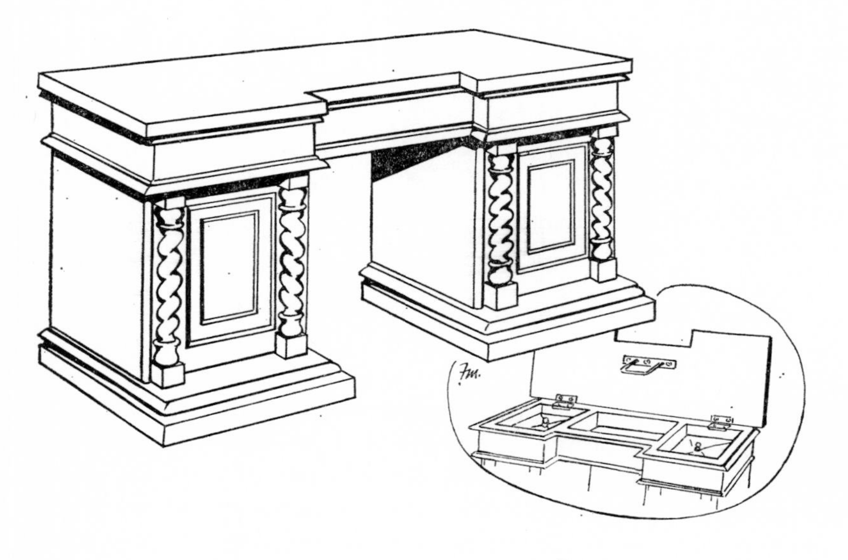

Fig. 13. Formed as a miniature sideboard: a mahogany Tea-caddy from the second quarter of the 19th century. (*Author*)

5

Broadly speaking, the Great Exhibition of 1851 marks the period of Victorian ornateness, and that it did much to stimulate that not necessarily admirable trend is undeniable. That the Great Exhibition was of outstanding interest, an encouragement of enterprise, a stimulus to trade is as obvious as that its aesthetic influence left much to be desired. Without assailing what was genuinely worthwhile, earnest, adventurous, a latter-day observer may be pardoned for feeling that the pudding was over-egged, and a mighty lot of triviality too seriously taken. That is a view which the reader may adopt or reject in the light of personal study, and bearing in mind that exhibits once highly esteemed, later disdainfully rejected, could now be once again popular, if perhaps for other reasons than those current in 1851.

A disadvantage of highly publicized displays is that not a few artists and craftsmen, even more manufacturers and wholesalers, are not unnaturally disposed to contribute items likely to hold their own against competition. The tendency to work *for* exhibition, to produce things which may or may not be significant *outside* an exhibition, can have disastrous results. Happily, it is not universal. But in the reverent or merely sightseeing crowds thronging Hyde Park in 1851, there were, even then, some whose verdict was anything but cordial.

Among them was a lad in his teens who surveyed the massed array of marvels with a rebellious eye. His name was William Morris.

6

Morris (1834–1896) is one of those commanding figures about whom one has to make up one's mind. That he was a great man is as evident as that the legacy of his talents was far-reaching and potent. All this is history. Yet, somehow and speaking for myself, one feels a need to take him down and dust him carefully, before replacing his image in its craftsmanlike niche. It is not easy now to appreciate how disturbing, how *new*, was the impact of the ideals he sponsored and unflinchingly practised; bearing in mind that a substantial part of their newness was focused on antiquity; or rather on his particular vision of a crafts-governed past projecting itself into a crafts-governed present and future. On Morris as a founder of Socialism in England, a socialism in its way as personal as everything else in this amazing man's repertoire, this is no place to linger. In my own (scarcely popular) view, the less workers in the arts embroil themselves in politics of any complexion, the better for their art. But Morris had not merely a finger but whole fists in so many pies as to prepare one for anything. And therein lies the trouble. Morris's shock value has dimmed; it is now in perspective, though perhaps not yet quite long enough a perspective for its complete understanding by the world at large. From creating a revolution, Morris became an episode. Yet his spirit still moves on the face of the waters.

Painting, typography, prose and verse, stained glass, furniture, metalwork, the designing of wallpapers, the weaving of carpets and other textiles – virtually the length and breadth of craftsmanship, coupled with the foundation of the Kelmscott Press, the Society for the Protection of Ancient Buildings, the Art-Workers' Guild – all these, and more, were virtually summed up in this burly man and his associates, this William Morris who so passionately denied the threat of the machine, and to whom craftsmanship was the quintessence of art.

Much in the more typically Victorian arts and crafts was heading, ever more violently, towards commercial triviality. True craftsmanship was dying, taste was degenerating, the old dignity of life was going by the board, and the Victorian Gadarene swine were hurtling to destruction in a sea of vulgarity. Such (more or less) was the view of Morris and his kind, and that it was not without substance is plain. Here, in effect, and however stale and mannered some of its manifestations may seem nowadays, was where Morris's revolt came in: a search for beauty alone, but for beauty on the best principles as envisaged by him and others of his temper. It was, to a dangerous degree, sincere and self-conscious, and therein lay the seeds of its latent dowdiness. In his own day, William Morris was to some a prophet, to others a dangerous innovator; he has passed into legend.

Fig. 14. As hated by William Morris, but now collectable: some 'showy' table-wares (*Mrs F. Gordon Roe*)

Fig. 15. Transfer ('Royal Arms') mark under a 'showy' IRONSTONE CHINA Gravy tureen, here upturned (*Mrs F. Gordon Roe*)

One may (and should) exercise as much discrimination in assessing the influence of Morris as in any other form of appreciation; but, whatever the outcome, the image of Morris in his niche is that of an outstanding personality in the annals of British art.

7

But this is anticipating. The firm of Morris, Marshall, Faulkner & Co., which gave practical shape to so many ideals, was only formed in 1861: the year before that of, so to call it, the 'Second Great Exhibition', meant for 1861 but deferred on account of one of those international upsets which crop up to spoil anything cultural.

If less remembered than its predecessor of 1851, the International Exhibition of 1862 is also an index to the progress of taste in Victorian England. It demonstrated the need for such a reaction as that of Morris and his circle. On its cultural side, the exhibition's tone was still much on the note of a superb and opulent pomposity. The highest technical perfection was lavished on things which, in our own day, might qualify as tycoon-taste, large, ornate, no-expense-spared. Costly-looking vases from Sèvres, with equally costly-looking essays in similar vein as interpreted by Minton, Copeland, and others, gave the fullest effect of finished performance and value for money, albeit Minton's *Henri II* ware is, at its best, not unpleasingly retrospective. Podsnappery in the crafts was still in the ascendant despite the earnest efforts of men such as William Burges, whose profoundly sincere Gothic cabinet of 1858, with painted decorations by E. J. Poynter, was all-of-a-piece with Burges's red-brick Tower House in the leafy shades of Melbury Road.

His was a personalized Gothic with strong nineteenth-century inflexions; but the cabinet, with affinities to a medieval *chasse*, is certainly not without character, to which Poynter's capable paintings of scenes from the *Legend of Cadmus* add a contrasting note by being rendered in a purely classical vein. To purists, the overall effect may seem a little odd; but so do the eighteenth-century Classico-Gothic towers of Westminster Abbey Church.

Fig. 16. Mid-Victorian chairs in contrasting styles, both suited to voluminously-skirted users: (L) a fashionable item from the 1860s perhaps by the London firm of G. M. & H. J. Story (*Mr and Mrs M. Maynard*), challenging an earlier, shapely, long-lived 'spoon-back' type. (*Mr and Mrs A. Spencer*)

Yet the *Cadmus* cabinet is far more Gothic in character than is Seddon's *King René's Honeymoon Cabinet* (1861) which, like Burges's of 1858, was also shown in the '62 Exhibition, and is now a familiar feature of the Victoria and Albert Museum. But whereas the *Cadmus* cabinet is in form unmistakably Gothic, the *René* is of typically Victorian build with vaguely Gothic embellishments. Its paintings, by a conglomeration of Burne-Jones, Rossetti, Madox Brown and Morris do nothing to dispel this impression. Their Gothicism is Pre-Raphaelite romantic, telling of a prithee age that never was, when (with certain monstrous exceptions) knyghtes were bold and tender, when chivalrie ruled, and (again with exceptions) fayre ladyes were gentil and wilted around in divers degrees of becoming Intensity. In short, it bore less relation to past actuality than did the 'Kiss Mammy', 'Sick Child' and 'Baby Blackleg' brands of domestic painting and portraiture to the realities of their own day.

Need these terms be explained? Surely not 'Kiss Mammy' that quintessence of sentimentality, nor, one detail apart, its near relative 'Sick Child'; but 'Baby Blackleg' perhaps. It has nothing whatever to do with politics, strikes, or trade unions, but was a recognized term for a trend of the 1880s for 'little girl' subjects: little girls in nice mob-caps, frilly dresses, and a considerable vision of black-stockinged legs – 'long ebony legs *à la* Chippendale', to quote the catalogue of Harry Furniss's *Royal Academy: An Artistic Joke* (1887).

> 'Bah! Bah! Blackleg,
> Getting quite a school.
> With such specimens of "Art"
> Galleries are full.'

Thus jingled Harry Furniss; and, if the prospect is discouraging, there are essays in this *genre* that look well enough on the right kind of wall.

As to 'Sick Child', this became the distinguishing nickname of Joseph Clark, ROI, who made a hit with the first picture he exhibited at the R.A. It was called *The Sick Child*, and the year was 1857. But though his *genre* embraced other homely themes as well as that of ailing youth, Joseph became known in the profession as 'Sick Child Clark'. He should not be confused, nor is there cause to confuse him, with James Clark, RI, an admirable figure

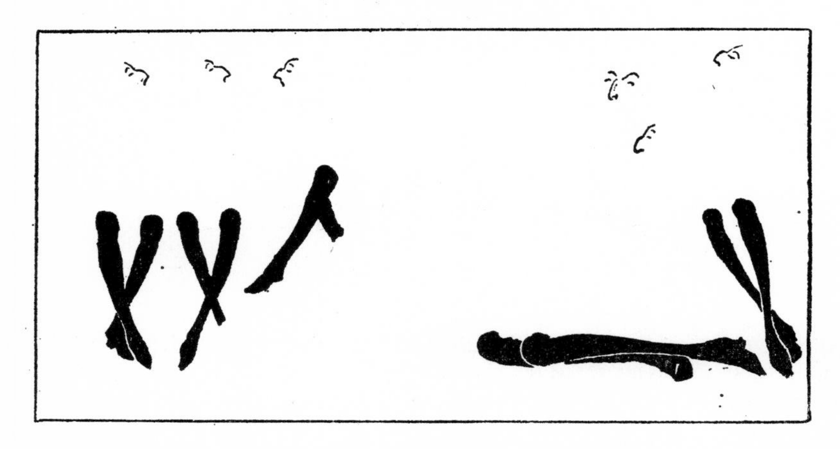

Fig. 17. 'Baby Blackleg' caricature from Harry Furniss's *Royal Academy: An Artistic Joke.*

painter, who was born in West Hartlepool in the year after that of his namesake's Academy debut. They were unrelated. 'Jimmy' Clark's art was completely unsentimental. In younger days he, H. H. La Thangue and certain fellow students returned from Paris so fancying their modernity as to call themselves 'The Bomb Throwers,' though in later years one might not have guessed it. La Thangue found his way to Royal Academicianship, though in 'Jimmy' Clark's case that distinction was reserved for his youngest son, my old friend Cosmo Clark, CBE. But this is leading us far away from the moods of Victorian Gothic.

8

It must not be supposed that interpreters of the Gothic and other retrospective styles invariably stuck as closely to their models as did, say, the Pugins or Burges. Charles Lock Eastlake, fourth son of the PRA of that name and himself Keeper of the National Gallery in 1855, is probably now best-known as creator of the 'Eastlake style' in furniture: a style which, if indebted to the past, more noticeably tended to use it as a spring-board for ideas. His *Hints*

7. The enormously spirited, thundering charge of the Greys in Lady Butler's *Scotland for Ever!* painted in 1881. (*Art Gallery and Temple Newsam House, Leeds*)

Orchardson's HER MOTHER'S VOICE, 1888 (*Tate Gallery*): more subtle in mood than some of his 'domestic' *tableaux*, of which Raymond Lister has acutely commented that 'We might almost be watching . . . a play by Pinero'. (*Victorian Narrative Paintings*, 1966)

8. Linley Sambourne's satire on J. C. Horsley, RA, as '*The Model British Matron*': 'Oh dear! Oh dear! Who could ha' sat for *that*?' From *Punch*, October 24, 1885. (By permission)

Martinware Vase with incised fish and water-weed pattern, dated 1887. (*William Morris Gallery, Walthamstow*)

9. *Morning Prayer*, by Francis Holl, ARA, after Edward Prentis. Of such were many middle-class homes at the start of Victoria's reign. Note the domestics seated at a distance—and the bulb-vases on the mantelshelf.

10. Gothic weds Classic. The 'Cadmus' Cabinet, designed by William Burges, made by Harland & Fisher, and decorated by E. J. Poynter (later PRA), 1858. (*Victoria and Albert Museum*)

C. F. A. Voysey, architect and designer: a prominent exponent of the Quaint Style. From a pencil sketch by Fred Roe, RI. (*Author*)

Fig. 18. A mid-Victorian Armchair of curvilinear quality, its underframing echoing 18th-century design. (*Belonging to Mr and Mrs A. Spencer*)

on Household Taste (1868) may have ceased to command the respect it formerly enjoyed, but Eastlake's, at times 'baronial', outlook created an important phase in the later Victorian furniture world. Rightly or wrongly one feels that whereas Eastlake was deliberately experimenting, Burges and Poynter had on this occasion seen nothing incongruous in commingling Greek and Gothic on the *Cadmus* cabinet. So too with a creditable oak cabinet designed in a modified Gothic by Philip Webb about 1865, and now at Walthamstow. Its painted panels by William De Morgan are, like Poynter's, in a classic vein – but Poynter wins!

9

When Poynter (1836–1919) painted the *Cadmus* decorations, he was in his early twenties, and had a long road to travel until, a baronet and GCVO, full of honours and, in more senses than one, academic distinctions, he was obliged by failing health to retire from the Presidency of the Royal Academy in December, 1918. In the July following, he died. Myself when young was once privileged, at a Royal Academy soirée, to exchange a silent handshake with this dignified elder, noting, as I did so, the thick lenses to his spectacles, for by then his sight was much impaired. Which lends point to a queer little story told to me by an artist I knew very well, and which, if 'out of period', is anything but out of context.

It is presumably in the July of 1919 that my artist (let me call him Alpha) chances to be near the lower end of Church Street, Kensington, since renamed Kensington Church Street. Observant, as becomes his vocation, he notices a figure walking on the opposite pavement, and recognizes Poynter. Recognition is not only of the familiar, bearded face, and thick-lensed glasses, but of the fur-collared coat which he had seen Poynter wearing before – and if this is July, what of it?

Punctilious in such matters, Alpha raises his hat to the official head of his profession. Becoming aware of the gesture, the old man peers across, lifts a hand in salute. And so passes on. . . .

Not much later, Alpha visiting an old friend, a member of the Royal Academy, casually mentions that he saw Poynter in Church Street, the other day. Becomes conscious that friend-RA is staring at him.

'*You saw Poynter in Church Street! Don't you know he is dying. He couldn't have been out.*'

Sure enough, the old Past-President did die at his home in Addison Road, for a sick man a fairish step from Kensington Church Street, on the morning of Saturday, July 26, 1919.

As for the story – sincerely told – was someone mistaken? Or is Church Street a way to Eternity?

FOUR

Art Nouveau, Beardsley (and What Not)

'Nothing is so dangerous as being too modern. One is apt to grow old-fashioned quite suddenly.' OSCAR WILDE

I

THERE are two brands of revolution, Promethean and Epimethean, and William Morris found inspiration in the past. Not in copying or in reconstructing it, but in adopting and adapting its methods and principles. Here again, in different guise, can be traced that living in a diluted projection of the past which appealed to the realist costume-painters. That Morris's designs were freed from the tortured intricacies of High Victorian opulence does not mean that his art was bare of all detail or even intricacy. Far from it. But contrasted with such elaborate fantasies as the 'Shakespeare Sideboard' of 1862 (now at Gateshead), a miracle of misplaced technical skill attributed to Gerrard Robinson (1834–91) to whom, by the way, Seymour Lucas had, when quite young, been apprenticed;[24] contrasted with so amazingly 'pictorial' a piece of wood-sculpture as this, or with Robinson's disastrous 'Robinson Crusoe' Sideboard (Victoria and Albert Museum), even the more elaborate of Morris's works were simplicity itself. They had, too, a grace which, if at times self-conscious, was a relief from Philistinian fussiness.

So, too, with a plain type of rush-seated chair or settee, of light build, blackened and with a row of turned bobbins set in its top back-rails. Graceful and strong, such chairs agreed well with the Aesthetic Movement. But the fact remains that they revived a type popular in the early part of the nineteenth century. What Morris's firm had done was successfully to adapt an old design in terms of modern requirements. Such interpretations are justified; but just how playful the more wilful forms of quaintness could be in other quarters is well seen in a four-page folder on good paper, issued by C. Hindley & Sons, of Oxford Street, London, 'Near to ye Cavendish Square', and printed by Faulkner, Manchester, in May 1880.

The whole thing, conceived in terms of the pseudo-antique, and addressed 'To Ye ART-LOVING PUBLICK', advertised Hindley's 'very greate stock' of Brussels Carpets, English Chintzes, Plain and 'Artistick' Furniture, and so forth, not forgetting Art Pottery, dear to aesthetes of the period, and presenting 'LINTHORPE, DUNMORE, JAPANESE, & VALLOURIE, in quaint and effective Shapes and Colours'. A detail on which one lingers nowadays is an offer of English Furniture Chintzes 'at lower Prices than ever previoufly, from 9d to 2/– per yard for beft Patterns, and *half-price* for REMNANTS & SHORT LENGTHS'. Mention of

[24] Marion H. Spielmann: *Seymour Lucas, RA, An Autobiographical Fragment* (in *The Times*, Weekly Edition, May 17, 1923).

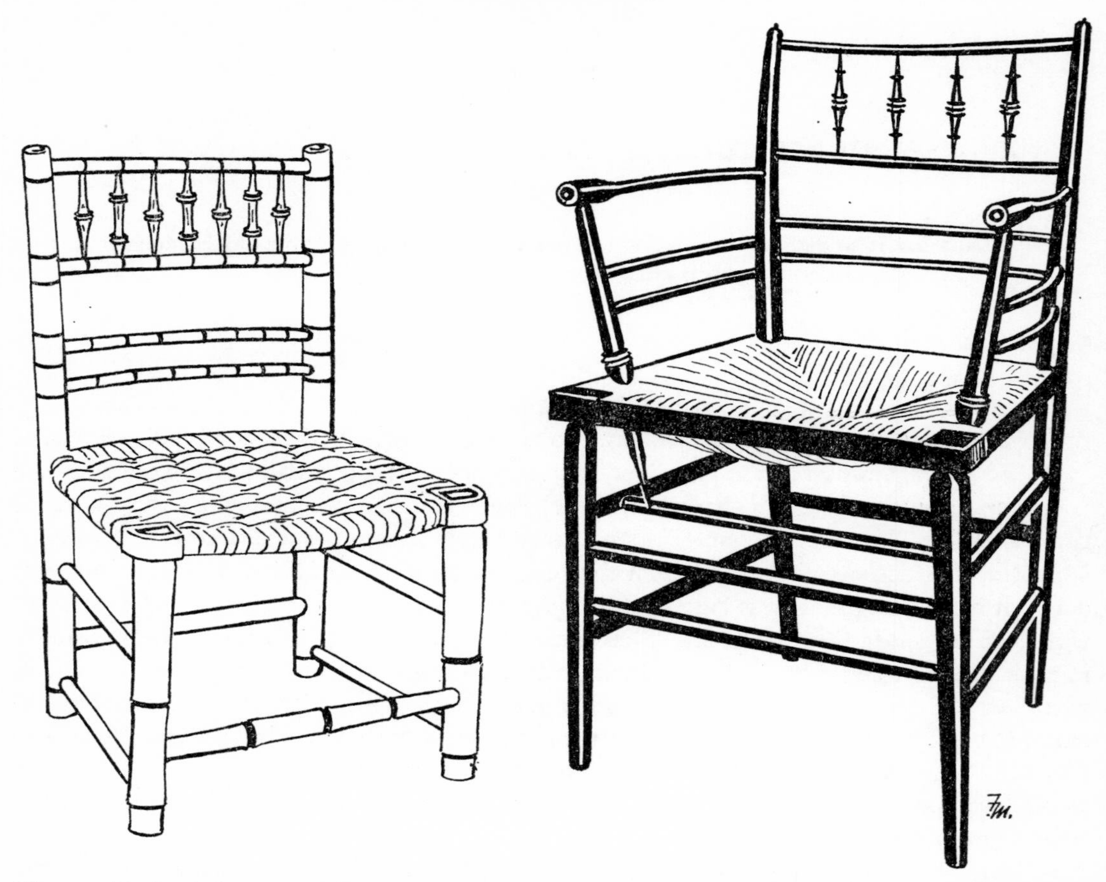

Fig. 19. Evolved from a widely distributed type, of which (L) is an early 19th-century example (*Mrs M. Maynard*), a rush-seated 'Sussex' armchair by Morris & Co. (*By permission of the William Morris Gallery, Walthamstow.*)

'MANTEL PIECES in Oak, Walnut, Mahogany and Black', reminds us of a traditional feature now being eliminated from many a room.

It is misleadingly easy to dismiss such circulars as well-meant, if slightly asinine, jokes; but such was not truly the case. They were Quaint, in the sense that *Art Nouveau* and its offshoots were Quaint; for though, when its freshness wore off, *Art Nouveau* came to be looked on as a pretty bad joke, it began as an authentic art form and, after a long lapse in aesthetic limbo, is now being fished out and restudied.

For its merits where these exist, one may add; as though at their best *Art Nouveau* and the Quaint Style evolved from it are inventively gracile and stimulating, at their worst they are howling absurdities. Indeed some of the less admirable furniture so defied the laws of practicability as to be more determinedly showy than normally or comfortably useful.

Just how far followers of *Art Nouveau* would gambol in an ecstasy of enthusiasm is well seen in Fig. 22, an extravaganza of 1896, elsewhere described by me as 'a drawing-room

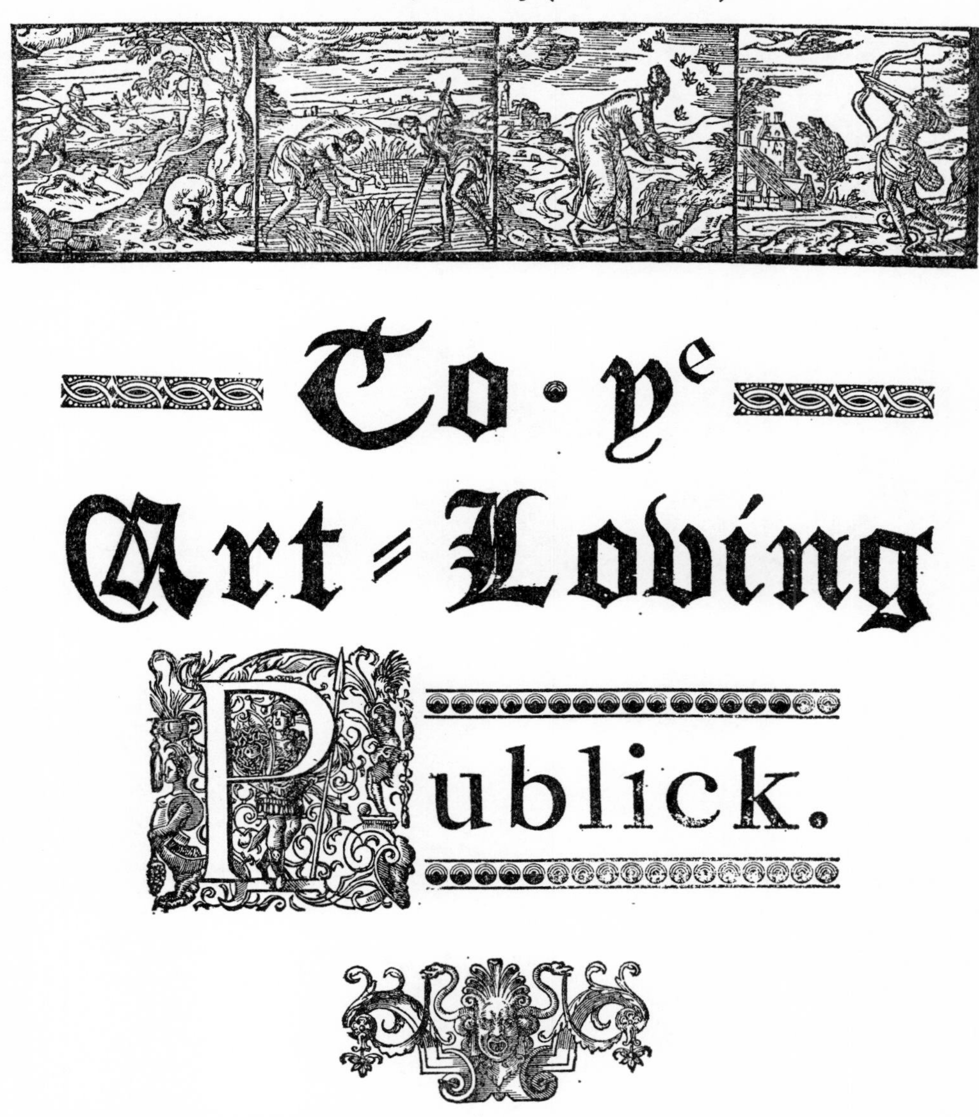

Fig. 20. In aesthetic-cum-antiquarian taste: detail from furnishing folder issued by C. Hindley & Sons, Oxford Street, London, May 1880.

affair such as might have been dreamed of by a Windsor chairmaker with illusions of grandeur'. It has the fascination of eccentricity, but what is of moment to students is that, for all his *fin-de-siècle* enthusiasm, its designer could not escape an eighteenth-century influence.

There are objections to describing this present discussion of *Art Nouveau* as an Animadversion on the Anatomy of Squirms.

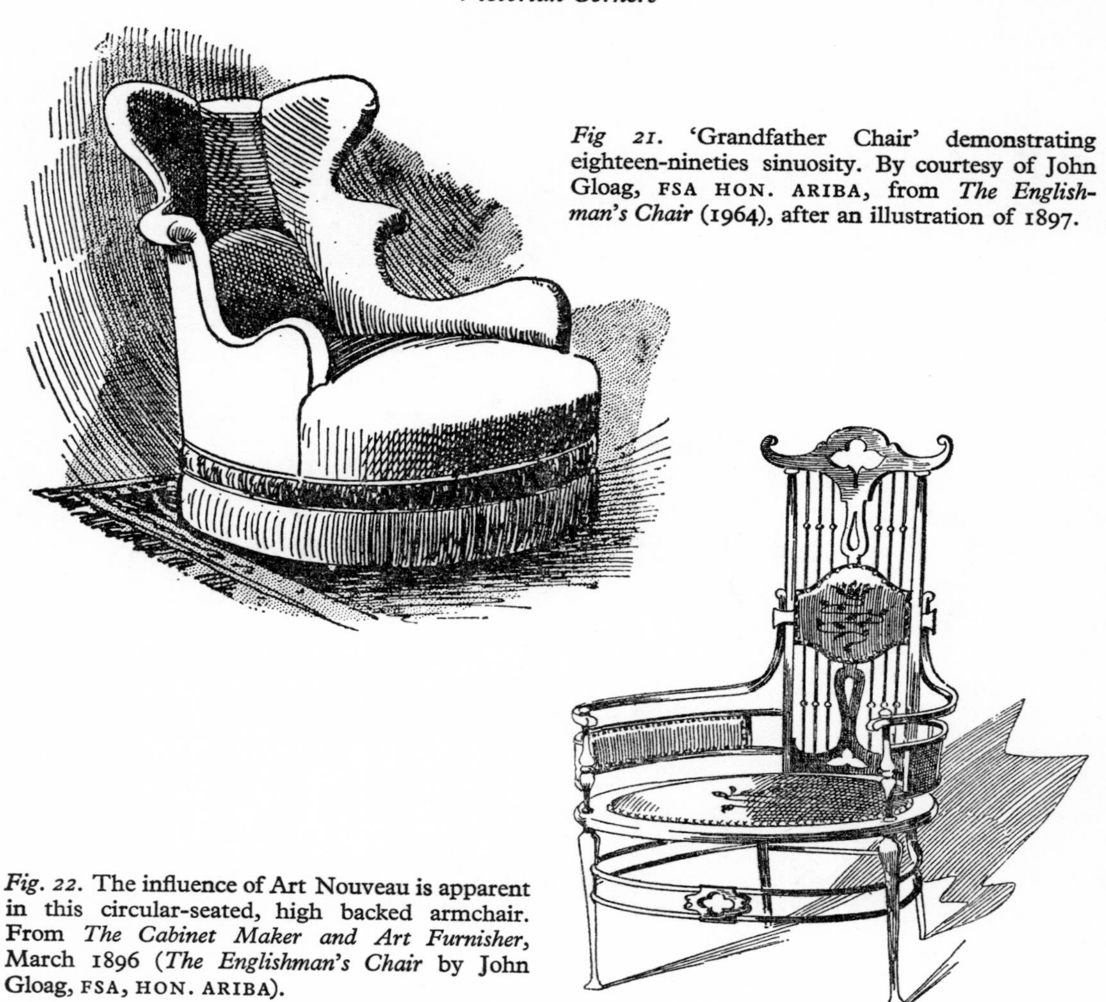

Fig 21. 'Grandfather Chair' demonstrating eighteen-nineties sinuosity. By courtesy of John Gloag, FSA HON. ARIBA, from *The Englishman's Chair* (1964), after an illustration of 1897.

Fig. 22. The influence of Art Nouveau is apparent in this circular-seated, high backed armchair. From *The Cabinet Maker and Art Furnisher*, March 1896 (*The Englishman's Chair* by John Gloag, FSA, HON. ARIBA).

2

If Morris himself felt no particular need for comfort in seating, he at least saw seating in terms of comely proportion, whereas a good many of those who came after him were arty-crafty at all costs. One is irresistibly reminded of Barry Pain's noxious little suburbanite in *The One Before* (1902) whose liking for fretwork inspired him to the making of an ornamental wheelbarrow (for the mantelpiece). 'In so far as that wheelbarrow could have been of no earthly use to anybody for anything, it may be considered to have been an instance of art for art's sake.' Not that all furniture of 'original' design was absurd. In his valuable book *The Englishman's Chair*, John Gloag is properly at pains to separate C. F. A. Voysey, and others of his temper, from the arty-crafty goats. Whether Voysey's work was always to one's personal taste is beside the point. An architect, he was an original thinker who knew that original thinking and practical expression must go hand-in-hand. As John Gloag has said of him: 'He was one of the first authentic modern designers.'

In my mind's eye, I can still see Voysey (1857–1941) in his accustomed seat near a sculptured marble fireplace in the Arts Club: Voysey with his clean-shaven, hawklike features, his spruce blue lounge suit cut, to his special instructions, without a turnover collar. And maybe I regret that I did not make more of my opportunities to cultivate so distinguished a senior.

Though Voysey's debt to Morris was less enduring than Ernest Gimson's, we have in Gimson again a designer of genuine consequence, and one who, like Morris, thought it no shame to adapt from the past that which he saw was good. His sense of proportion, of clean, sound structural line, of that restraint which is the true squire of knowledge – such qualities have made Gimson memorable beyond his own age.

But with Gimson we have got right away from *Art Nouveau.*

3

Though (to quote Brian Reade's penetrating analysis) *Art Nouveau* 'nominally' began 'with an exhibition at Bing's *Maison de l'Art Nouveau* in Paris in 1895',[25] it had been 'in the air'. In some indefinable way, the time was ripe for it. If its origins are Continental, one is prepared for the *art nouveau* explosion by elements in Morris's designs; and though nobody would identify Sir Alfred Gilbert as an *art-nouveau* sculptor, one has only to look at the arabesque details of the base of his Shaftesbury Memorial Fountain, the world-renowned 'Eros' in Piccadilly Circus, or the convolutions of his *Tomb of H.R.H. The Duke of Clarence* at Windsor, to realize what could be done in this way by a genius. And both these works, to name them alone, were begun, and, in Eros's case finished, *before* the mode for *Art Nouveau* was fully established elsewhere. Not all Gilbert's work is conceived in a similar vein; it is this aspect only of it which comes into my argument; but in view of Eros's fame, we should pause and reflect that at first it encountered hostility, and that (as Gilbert's nephew, Adrian Bury, has recorded) it involved the sculptor in such ruin and anguish as to brand it forever with him as his 'Evil Genius'.[26]

4

Morris (to return to him) was far greater as a designer than as a figure painter in a manner too often amounting to Middle-Ages-and-water. His original designs for 'Acanthus' wallpaper (1875; Victoria and Albert Museum) or for 'Avon' chintz (*c.* 1886; William Morris Gallery, Walthamstow) are commanding essays in convolutions, by a master hand. If a trifle too ornamented for every taste, his Kelmscott Press books are typographical masterpieces. His furniture – and there was much more to it than the bobbin-back chairs previously mentioned – shows superb craftsmanship. Morris was a dynamic personality, whose pure or diluted influence penetrated into what may be called the 'cosy-corner' period and beyond. H. G. Wells' 'Miss Winchelsea' was of her age in imagining 'a refined little home, with two bureaus,

[25] Brian Reade: *Art Nouveau and Alphonse Mucha* (HMSO, 1963; 2nd ed. 1966).

[26] Adrian Bury: *Shadow of Eros* (Dropmore Press, 1952).

with white shelves of high-class books, and autotypes of the pictures of Rossetti and Burne-Jones, with Morris's wall-papers and flowers in pots of beaten copper'.

Refinement, of course, was much in the minds of those who thought in terms of culture without having experienced creative passion. With Morris it was different, with the Pre-Raphaelites it was different, with all artists worthy the name, and whatever their *genre*, it was different. And yet there is something dead about much of the work that once seemed so 'new' to us (or to our fathers). Was it perhaps always so? When all is said, it was Browning who, in his own day, gave the last word about the Rossetti-like type:

> 'Dear dead women, with such hair too –
> what's become of all the gold
> Used to hang and brush their bosoms?
> I feel chilly and grown old.'

But there was an artist, of a very different temper, whose short but crowded life left him no room in which to lament the onset of age. Aubrey Beardsley.

5

It escapes my memory why my good friend and sometime colleague Herbert Granville Fell, with his direct experience of the arts in late Victorian England, should have distrusted so well avouched a story as that of Whistler's meeting with Aubrey Beardsley. It is a familiar tale: Whistler eyeing Beardsley's drawings for *The Rape of the Lock* (published 1896) aloofly – interestedly – enthusiastically; finally admitting that he had 'made a very great mistake', and that the, by now weeping, young man was 'a very great artist'. It was one of the most generous gestures Whistler ever made. Admittedly, Granville Fell's incredulity was not voiced (to my knowledge) *ex cathedra;* nor is there need to enhance the fame of Beardsley. Any suspicion of dowdiness that had cobwebbed around his art was blown away in 1966 by the Aubrey Beardsley Exhibition at the Victoria and Albert Museum, by far the most comprehensive display so far assembled of his *œuvre*. That those not *aficionados* should at one time have become a trifle tolerant of Beardsley, instead of either acclaiming him to the aesthetic heavens or (more characteristically) consigning him to every circle of damnation, is merely another instance of the ups-and-downs of taste. The savage execration aroused by his art has dwindled; and though it may be felt that, unlike some, Beardsley (or rather his art) has had to wear less than many another the shabby mantle of outmoded modernism, he is now seen without bias and anew. If the 'Beardsley period' – to which Max Beerbohm (in his urbanity) claimed to belong – was an incident within an episode, its influence was at once bold and tentaculate.

6

That Beardsley (1872–98) was a remarkable artist in black-and-white has always been inescapable. That, bias apart, there was substance in the claim that there was what Victorians would have called an 'unpleasant' side to his personality and that this kink outcropped in his art, not necessarily in detail but as it were in feeling, is also evident. The distinction is that of certain things in one of Chesterton's *Father Brown* stories not being 'the right shape'. That Beardsley's shapes were often of great beauty does not always make them 'right'. To assume an equation between Greatness and Goodness is always dangerous.

How King Arthur saw the Questing Beast (1893) is by any standard an amazingly able drawing, as is that much-reproduced work *The Peacock Skirt* for Wilde's *Salome* (1894), to mention but two of many. But some there are of which it is idle to deny that a superb technique has been devoted to unworthy ends; and if that sounds Ruskinian, it is, in my opinion, true. That Beardsley could be, one might say, fiendishly clever is patent; but that his skill amounts to genius is beyond cavil.

Like Frederick Walker, so unlike him in other respects, Beardsley came of a family of jewellers, a point worth noting in view of the two men's leanings to techniques 'curiously wrought'. Beardsley's decorative sense, his sure sweep of sinuous line, his daring use of solid blacks are always impressive. Even now, when their first impact has passed, the sheer skill of his drawings is arresting. Small wonder that such qualities exerted a considerable influence on illustration and design; small wonder, too, that Beardsley's work should have received the dubious accolade of being not merely imitated but forged. It is when one contrasts the true with the derivative that one realizes to the full how sure was Beardsley's touch. Indeed, and regarding his work without reference to biographical or gossiping notices of its creator, we find that where Beardsley, so different from most other Victorians and by most so condemned, makes his initial appeal to us is by that very command of technique which is in itself a basic quality of much Victorian art.

Even so, that wild death-cry of his, urging the destruction of 'By all that is holy *all* obscene drawings' confesses an appalling moment of truth.

7

And all the while, with revolutions raging in paint, illustration, and in verse, with Morris creating his own brave new world in which William De Morgan's scholarly pottery, inspired by Persian motifs, played so conspicuous a part; all the while, not only furniture but all manner of things of unmistakably and even dowdily 'Victorian' stamp were made and used – and went on being used long after any novelty that may have been theirs had gone by the board. Their traces are everywhere – as in the case of the carved wood object in what may be called the 'railway-Gothic' taste of the 1860s (Fig 23), made as the stand for a circular clock, not (one suspects) of first quality.

In *The Idle Thoughts of an Idle Fellow* (1889), Jerome K. Jerome amusingly toyed with the notion that: 'There must surely be some special and secret manufactory for the production of lodging-house ornaments . . . . *never seen anywhere else.*' It is not, of course, true though there were moments when it almost seemed feasible. He instances the lustres, 'one at each end of the mantel-piece, where they are never safe'; they being 'hung around with long triangular slips of glass that clank . . . . and make you nervous'. (Not that lustres, by then outdated, were peculiar to 'digs'.) Above all, Jerome notes

Fig. 23. Stray wood-carvings: a mid-nineteenth century *putto*, found in a corner near Swiss Cottage; and (*below*) a clock-base in railway-Gothic taste of about the 1860s (*Mr. Philip G. Maynard*)

'In the commoner class of rooms, ... a couple of pieces of china which might each be meant to represent a cow sitting upon its hind legs, or a model of the temple of Diana at Ephesus, or a dog, or anything else you like to fancy.'

Perhaps dog, one of the squatting, spaniel-like type known as 'Comforter', is what Jerome really meant, as these pottery ornaments had not yet been raised from a common or cottagey status to the enlightened appreciation bestowed equally, and at times more deservingly, on those spirited figures, the Staffordshire 'flats'.

By more recent standards, Jerome's pen-picture of even respectable furnished lodgings is grim, though it has more in it for neo-Victorians than Wells's brief but effective impression of Madam Gadow's apartments in *Love and Mr Lewisham* (1900). From this I merely instance the 'two toilet tidies used as ornaments', instead of in their appointed place on the dressing-table.

As a latter-day collector may murmur: there are tidies and tidies. In my past, toilet or hair tidies were usual. More often than not, they were cylindrical affairs of pottery with a circular hole in the lid, through which combings, wound round a finger, were swiftly and easily lodged. Some tidies were plain, some ornamental. I once picked up a decidedly odd one; there are moments when trivialities assume an importance.

Fig. 24. Dignity (a stylish glass Lustre) and Impudence ('cottagey' pottery ornaments). (Various)

Fig. 25. One of various types of Staffordshire 'Comforter' dogs.

Hurrying over such details as that the ware is English of *circa* 1850, that it bears the pattern name KENILWORTH, and that the relief decoration has been overlaid with transfer ornament, we come to the main point of interest. The formal blue transfer pattern is relieved by two scenes, one of a stock rural cottage and stream, the other an unrelated military item. A private with a weight, or possibly a pack, strapped to his back, is bending over a late-type Windsor chair, while behind him stands a monocled officer, in military tunic and shako, holding a shovel. Below is the legend: SMITH. 9th HALF. MILITARY DISCIPLINE. Why such a scene should be figured on a hair-tidy, or what was the background of the incident, real, reputed, propagandist or would-be satirical, has escaped my inquiry.

Such an item is curious, though for a trifle at once maturer and less uncomfortable a small,

Fig. 26. 'Military Discipline' satire on a Hair Tidy of *circa* 1850. (*Mr Michael Maynard, M.I.Mech.E.*)

Fig. 27. Olive-green dish with turqoise 'print' in the 'Intense' taste of about 1880 (*Author*)

whorl-shaped olive-green dish with a turquoise-coloured 'print' may be preferred (Fig 25). This production of *circa* 1880, is not only typical pottery of its period. It evokes mental pictures of heavy curtains and bobble-trimmed drapes; and suggests in its central device the aim and ambition of so many young women of its day: to look as much like Ellen Terry as nature – and art – would allow.

FIVE

Of Ravens and Writing-desks

'"Curiouser and curiouser!" cried Alice.' LEWIS CARROLL

I

GIVEN time, inclination, and firm contract, I might turn out a passable book on the English pun. Plays on words have a very long history. Our classical and medieval forefathers relished them; so too, in their day, did Shakespeare and many another. They crop up in speech, verse, and prose. We find them in armory; we find them on tombstones; we find them, superlatively, in Priestman Atkinson's ('Dumb Crambo Junior's') quaint little 'funnies' in *Punch.*

When it comes to Victorian puns – and not every Victorian pun was coined in the Victorian age – there is a vast store of material, much of it in riddle-form, ranging from the simple:

> 'What is the difference between an accepted and a rejected lover?
> One kisses his missis, the other misses his kisses.'

– to riddles involving such a piling of Pelion on Ossa of puns as to render the hapless listener rigid with boredom. Not counting fireworks from Thomas Hood or the less kindly Douglas Jerrold, one has only to dip into that determinedly facetious book *Puniana,* edited by the Hon. Hugh Rowley, and first published in 1867, to savour the fullness of what was, in its day, a very popular form of wit. So much so, that Rowley (late 16th Hussars and a younger son of the 2nd Lord Langford) was encouraged to issue *More Puniana* in 1875.

As a cicerone to sheer, naked, unashamed punning, Rowley is as unsurpassed as no matter; but it was not unknown for private collections to be kept in manuscript. One, compiled by my grand-aunt Ada, gave me joy in my very young days. At a guess it was put together in the 1880s, 'from various sources', and whether those sources were conversational or printed ('so amusing, you know') matters not. So industrious a collector of such trifles was grand-aunt Ada that she even found space for the Mad Hatter's poser, 'Why is a raven like a writing-desk?', thoughtfully appending the comment 'There is no answer'.

What a good many people (besides grand-aunt Ada) overlooked is that, in later years, Lewis Carroll himself tried to answer his own impossible riddle. So often was he asked about it that, in self-defence, he eventually devised what he called 'a fairly appropriate answer', to be found in the Preface of the 1896 edition of *Alice's Adventures in Wonderland*: 'Because it can produce a few notes, though they are *very* flat; and it is never put with the wrong end in front.' Carroll himself did not think well of this laboured effort, and we may agree with him. It savours less of whimsicality than of midnight oil. Originally, 'Why is a raven . . . .' was never meant to be answered. In any true sense, it never was. We are left raven-ous. . . .

Fig. 28. Writing-desk in action. From *The Adventures of Mr Verdant Green.* (1853)

All the same, what exactly had Carroll in mind when speaking here of a writing-desk? That he himself owned one is on record. A writing-desk authenticated as having been used by him was in the Lewis Carroll Centenary Exhibition, organized by J. & E. Bumpus Ltd in 1932. The catalogue describes it as being of mahogany, $13\frac{1}{2} \times 10 \times 5\frac{1}{2}$ in. when shut. Portable writing-desks were of more than one type, from the simple slope with a box-interior, to the

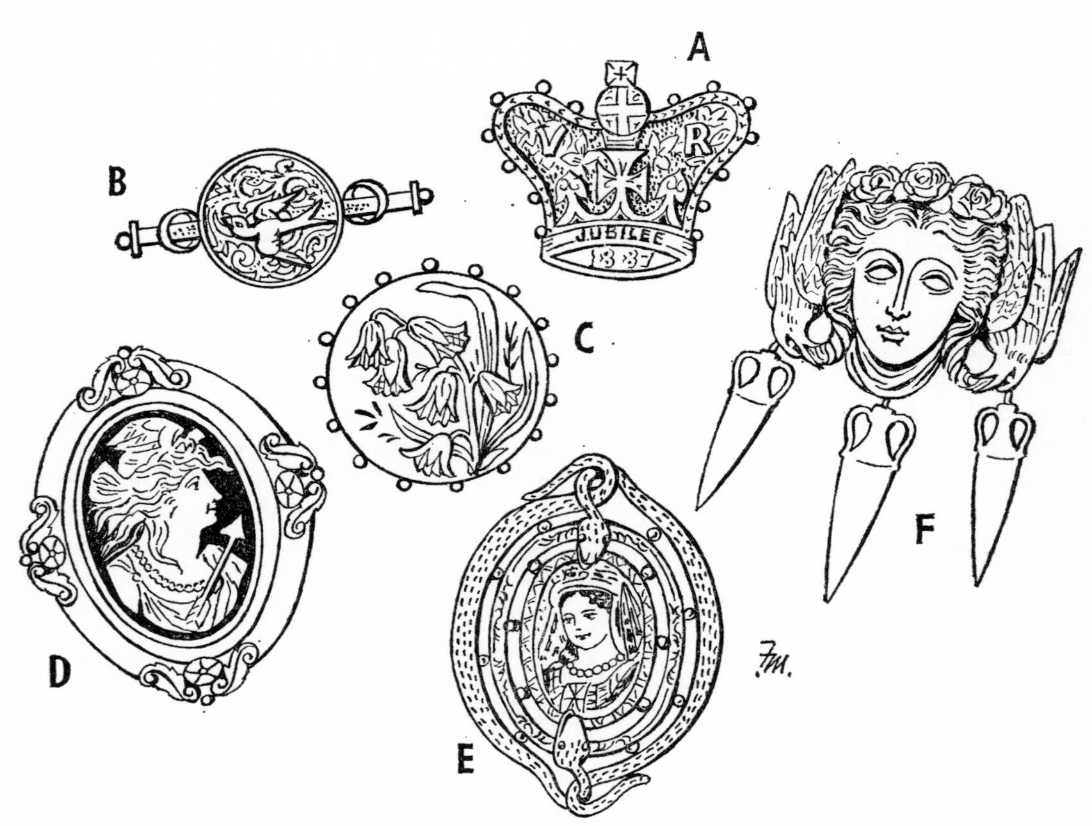

Fig. 29. From Victorian jewel cases: 'Everyday' brooches of various dates. (A) 'V. R. JUBILEE 1887', silver, part gilt, Birmingham 1886-7 (*Miss Cecelia Neville*); (B) silver, Birmingham, 1896; (C) silver unmarked; (D) 'Diana' shell cameo in 'pinchbeck' mount; (E) silvered brass with enamel miniature; (F) carved blue grey lava. (*Mrs M. Maynard*)

elaborate, rectangular casket, unfolding to form a slope, leathered or otherwise, with storage space beneath, and sundry refinements conducive to correct correspondence. Old fiction abounds in mentions of heroes or heroines getting out their writing-desks, and, if with no very sound reason, I like to imagine that the more elaborate kind at least has a footing in *Wonderland.*

For one thing, this very book on *Victorian Corners* was written on just such a desk, given to me by two dear folk for the better discipline of my literary litter. It is a superior desk, brass-bound, leathered and gilt-stamped within, and possessing its secret place, as was not uncommon in 'better' examples. The desk folds up and locks up, has its own little brass-stoppered inkpot, a curved tray for pens and a small sloped-bottomed compartment for wafers or postage stamps. Both tray and sloped-bottom are removable, revealing additional space, that under the diagonal housing a spring operating the 'secret'.

What small mysteries or treasures such 'hides' once harboured provokes speculation. Love-letters, love-gages, perchance? Trinkets 'too good' to be left lying about? Jewel cases, too, had often their 'secrets', though whether it occurred to their owners that it would be a great deal simpler for a scoundrel to snatch the whole box than to waste time in a pottering search for masked 'hides', is no business of ours.

So, let us assume that this handsome desk of mine holds more than the muddle of stationery, used but re-usable envelopes, pieces of scrap paper, odd drafts of discarded paragraphs, and hopelessly mislaid memoranda. Let us see this desk of mine as a species of lucky-dip laid bare to your curiosity.

2

First of all, this seal. I have several and use them; for the seemly old business of sealing a letter with one's signet, or some other comely device, is not extinct as far as my private correspondence is concerned. That red splash on the back of a letter, bedight with such insignia as one has at command, gives a pleasurable boost to one's ego, and tells one's friends one esteems them enough to take that much more trouble in addressing them.

Next, let us suppose we turn up a number of Victorian Christmas cards (*v.y.* as bibliographers say), some of them commercial, others, small original water-colours; or maybe a De la Rue's neat little 'Finger Shape' Condensed Diary in slip-on case, with pencilled entry under July 28, 1882 – 'Saw a balloon go up'; and then a bundle of old *carte-de-visite* photographs of whiskered men and voluminous women, reminding us that, back in 1853, a magazine called *The Family Friend* had published a number of articles on *Practical Instructions in the Art of Photography*; a subject still novel enough to warrant an explanatory footnote:

'The word Photography is pronounced thus, Fo-tog-graffy – the accent on the second *o* being pronounced as the *o* in clog, not, cock, collar, con, concave, &c.'

3

But those Victorian Christmas cards earlier mentioned: a glance at them might be rewarding. One of them brings back to me an old priest-uncle of mine, to whom I was greatly attached.

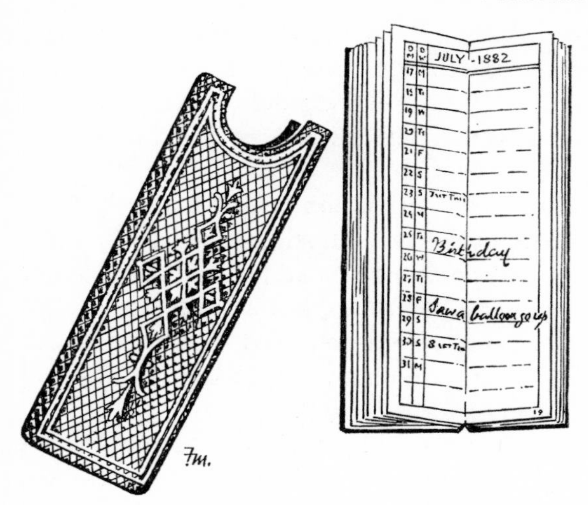

Fig 30. 'Adapted for the Pocket or Recticule': De la Rue 'Finger Shape' Condensed Diary for 1882 (H. 3¼ ins). (*In the Author's Collection*)

Fig 31. Gilt-metal Needle-case, issued by W. Avery & Son, Redditch, in the 1870s. (*Author*)

When quite a boy, he bought one of them for the sheer joy of it – about 1870, by the look of the card – and was so fascinated that he kept it till the day of his death. And small wonder, for here is one of those folding 'animated' or 'tableau' cards: on its front a scene of fashionable folk arriving for 'Ye Christmas Pantomime', at what could be meant for the T.R., Drury Lane, with red-coated guardsmen on duty. Opened, the house is seen, with an equally fashionable audience, and a cut-out proscenium complete with transformation scene and harlequinade in progress. Minute lettering gives the name of B[enjamin] Sulman, an active London publisher of such fancies from the early 1860s onwards.[27]

With this pleasing relic there turned up a little gilt metal easel, bearing the impressed stamp of W. AVERY & SON, REDDITCH, as well as the Registered Mark, which latter would give an exact date were it legible, and which in any case was discontinued after 1883.[28] The 'picture' on the easel is really a needle-case, closing with a snap-catch. Small packets of Sharp's Egg Eyed Needles (manufactured by Avery) are still within; the whole easel being cased in a white cardboard box, inscribed, in a youthful scrawl, 'With Charlie's love to dear Mamma wishing her a merry Christmas and a Happy New Year'. True to the sentiment of the age, the battery of needles appears to be more or less intact. Gifts from dear ones stood a chance of being preserved to the verge of fossilization. Were it otherwise, our knowledge of the Victorian past would be less intimate than it is.

I recall trifles in my mother's writing-desk: a perfectly fashioned pair of miniature gloves in blue kid for a doll, an equally minute hand-mirror, a bundle of tiny dolls' newspapers (French), an old dance-programme or so with pencil attached. Also letters which passed when she was engaged and which, some years after her death, I burned unread in a garden. Such things had long since become the husks of happy memories.

[27] George Buday: *The History of the Christmas Card* (ed. 1964).
[28] See Roe: *Victorian Furniture* (1952), and *Home Furnishing with Antiques* (1965).

11. Original design by William Morris for his 'Avon' chintz, *c.* 1886. (*William Morris Gallery*)

Some tiles in the William Morris Gallery, Walthamstow (left to right, top): 'Dragon', W. De Morgan; 'Beauty and the Beast', Burne-Jones; (below) 'Drake', Philip Webb; 'Cinderella', Burne-Jones—the last in strongly medieval mood

12. *The Toilet of Salomé*. Replacing a less restrained version, this drawing by Aubrey Beardsley was first illustrated in the 1894 edition of Wilde's *Salomé*. From the original, by courtesy of the British Museum

4

It was in another old desk that I came upon a tattered relic of the Cambridge of 1881: a printed programme of the sixteenth of the series of Penny Musical Entertainments, given by Members of Clare College on Saturday evenings in the Large Room at Cambridge Guildhall. In the nature of things, one doubts whether many copies of these programmes can have survived in private hands, kept, as this one must have been, for the words of the songs.

One, Macfarren's *My own, my Guiding Star* (sung by Mr O. Puckridge) impressed at least one listener, who pencilled a cross against it; but, unless I mistake the occasion, a rendering, by Mr W. H. Wing, of Sterndale Bennett's *'Tis Jolly to Hunt* had to be called off. 'As it's not jolly to hunt for a song you can't find, we will have something else'.

An easy impromptu.

5

But here is an oddment one would be lucky to find in a desk, as, in the specialized world of Carrolliana, it is a collector's item: THE WONDERLAND POSTAGE-STAMP CASE, 'Invented by Lewis Carroll MDCCCLXXXIX', though actually published by Emberlin & Son, Oxford, in 1890. This is a small case of stitched parchmenty paper with 12 pockets for stamps of denominations from ½d to 1/–. Outside are pictures in colours (after Tenniel) of Alice with the Pig, and of The Cheshire Cat vanishing. This case has a slip-on cover of paper printed with Alice with the Duchess' baby, and the Cheshire Cat on the branch. So by swiftly pulling the case from its cover, the transformation from babe to piglet, and from cat to grin is playfully achieved. 'Coloured Pictorial Surprises' is the description on yet another, covering envelope, though one may be excused for feeling that the 'surprises' verge on mildness.

With this stamp-case was provided a small duodecimo 40-page leaflet by Carroll himself: *Eight or Nine Wise Words about Letter-Writing*, which not only instructed the purchaser how to use the case, but how to write and register letters, with other timely information. Merely to issue a stamp-case without the addition of a useful and entertaining commentary was not at all Carroll's idea.

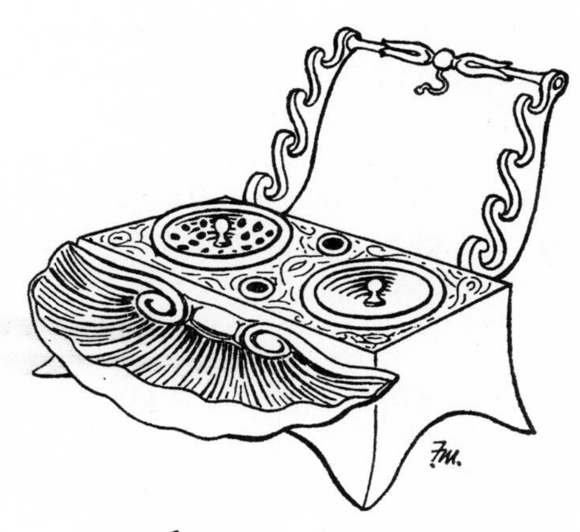

Fig. 32. With its pounce-pot, a (continental) bronze inkstand (H. 4 ins.) of *circa* 1855. (*Author*)

Eight editions of *Eight or Nine Words* are recorded, and sundry variations of the other items[29]; by when the elegant little bronze inkstand which flanks my writing-desk was anything but new (Fig. 32). One of its porcelain pots, with the Vienna mark for 1855, is still equipped with a dredger-cap for pounce. . . .

6

Perhaps the most outstanding item in Carrolliana, the prototype, more precisely one of the prototypes, of *Alice's Adventures in Wonderland* has become freely accessible in facsimile, with an able introduction by Martin Gardner. This version, called *Alice's Adventures Under Ground*, dates from 1864, and is of interest as much for its resemblances to, as its differences from, the final version of *Wonderland* published by Macmillan in 1865. But the 'Dover' facsimile, issued a century later, was not the first. Macmillan had put out one of *Alice's Adventures Under Ground* in 1886, a specimen page of which was tantalizingly featured in the advertisement section of later editions of the *Alice* books. This, the complete Macmillan facsimile of 1886, is now itself a collector's piece. What emerges from a comparison of *Under Ground* and *Wonderland* is how greatly the book had gained by re-writing and expansion. *Under Ground* is a chrysalid *Wonderland.*

It always puzzles me when a certain kind of peevish criticism is levelled at the *Alice* books. There was once a writer (I forget her name) who doubted whether children had ever really enjoyed *Alice;* suggesting that it was merely nostalgic glamour which made grown-ups believe that they had loved *Alice* when they too were young. In short, they were kidding themselves.

Perhaps yes – in certain, to my mind, unhappy cases; but in general, no. Speaking for myself, I have revelled in *Alice* since before I could read, and in my age wish to goodness I could write anything one tenth so alive. That the *Alice* books have vitality is plain. They are a true act of genius, whereas, in my opinion, Jonathan Miller's much discussed film of *Alice in Wonderland* (1966) can be summed up as – clever.

7

Quite a list of other derivatives could be adduced, though few of them have survived their initial furore. Leaving out of it such political skits as *Clara in Blunderland* and *The Westminster Alice* (both 1902), it is claimed by Gillian Avery that that once so popular book for the young, *The Wallypug of Why* (1895) and its successors by George Edward Farrow were heavily inspired by *Alice.*[30] It is scarcely excessive to suggest that, for a space at any rate, 'Wallypug' became a household word. *The Wallypug of Why* is a catchy title.

Not but what there were other ways in which the *Alice* influence made itself felt. It can be properly argued that various Alice-like figures in illustrations simply portrayed what Alice herself was, a nice little girl of the 1860s. All the same, and discounting obvious 'fetches',

[29] *A Handbook to the Literature of the Revd Charles Lutwidge Dodgson (Lewis Carroll)*, by S. H. Williams and Falconer Madan, revised to 1960 by Roger Lancelyn Green (O.U.P., 1962).

[30] Gillian Avery with the assistance of Angela Bull: *Nineteenth Century Children: Heroes and Heroines in English Children's Stories 1780–1900* (Hodder & Stoughton, 1965), p. 133.

Fig. 33. An *Alice*-type child from the Hon. Mrs Arthur Egerton's *Stories for Darlings* (John Murray, 1870)

there are drawings which give pause for thought. What of a diminutive Alice-like fairy in *Stories for Darlings* (John Murray), of which a copy of the second edition (1870) is to my hand.

This children's book – one could have wished for almost any other title – was written by the Hon. Mrs Arthur Egerton, youngest daughter of Martin Tucker Smith, MP, and wife of the fourth son of the 1st Earl of Ellesmere of the creation of 1846. As literature, it oozes affection, and it is just this one illustration from it that we need consider. In point of time, this comes between *Wonderland* (1865) and *Looking-Glass* (1872), as does the little girl's dress, etc. As I demonstrated in *The Victorian Child* (Phoenix, 1961), Alice's attire and hair styling differ slightly from one book to another. Here I refer to Tenniel's Alice, who again differs from Carroll's own, amateurish drawings in *Under Ground*, though Tenniel did borrow an idea or so from them.

Tenniel's contribution towards establishing the popular visual image of Alice is hugely important. When we liken (as we do to this day) some little long-tressed girl, blessed with the wrapt intentness of childhood, to an 'Alice-in-Wonderland', it is Tenniel's image that leaps to mind. The collaboration of Carroll and Tenniel was a union of genius. But without Carroll there would have been no Alice. In extolling Tenniel, than whom nobody has more expressively realized in line that endearing child of the ages, we pay homage to Lewis Carroll whose kindly hand has led generation upon generation of young and old alike to Wonderland and Through the Looking-Glass.

8

It was after those words were written, that happy circumstance led to what was, for me, an unexplored aspect of Looking-Glass Land. There is northwards of London, in Finchley, a gracious park called The Avenue, formed (like my own beloved Holland Park) from an ancient estate; and it was while contentedly rambling among old and squirrel-haunted trees that I and my companion came in sight of a large Victorian building, in a corner of the grounds, which, for one fleeting moment, almost made me expect to find Alice herself beside me.

There is here no visible sign of the ancient Temple Croft, once belonging to the Templars, and to the Hospitallers after them. Avenue House, now municipal offices, is of a typically Victorian vintage. But what caught my eye is that, at an after-date, improvements, ranging from Tudoresque to Norman (more or less in that order), had been added with striking effect.

Now, in *Looking-Glass*, Chapter Nine, in which Alice becomes a queen, there is Tenniel's well-known illustration of Alice talking to the very old Frog; and Tenniel has chosen to place them in front of a round-arched Norman doorway, complete with cushion capitals, dog's-tooth carving, and bulgeydingo strap-hinges.

Through the Looking-Glass was published in 1872; and I am not trying to force a relationship between Tenniel's drawing and the Romanesque amenities of Avenue House, which, it seems, belong to 1884, But what is material is that Tenniel, in designing a prideful background in key with Alice's royal state, had chosen an architectural revivalism which (if one can speak thus of anything so substantial) was again in the air – as it had been about 1840 – and which, in a measure, that very drawing of his could best encourage. As Mr Stephens saw no objection to carving his monogram or a Stephens crest of *a demi-spreadeagle* in the tympana of 'Norman-style' doorways – other armorials suitable to the name are about the house – we need not be too particular. If these were real Norman doorways, the conjunction would be odd enough; but in the Victorian age such anomalies excited no comment. Indeed we should gratefully remember Mr Stephens for leaving this haven of peace to the good folk of Finchley.

Mr Stephens? None less than Henry Charles Stephens, known locally as the 'uncrowned king of Finchley', and in the greater world as 'Inky Stephens' from the celebrated product which bears his name.

Here, in The Avenue at Finchley, is a Victorian corner replete with peace and beauty. . . . But, why *is* a raven like a writing-desk?

SIX

Of 'Fun', with 'Punch' and 'Judy'

'If you don't have fun in your studies, you'll get nothing but pedantry for a result.' WILLIAM HUNT

I

NOTHING (unless it be British politics) is harder to analyse than comic humour. One may quote favourite passages from *Alice* or the *Sylvie and Bruno* books, and find them diverting, but coldly to classify them in terms of antithesis, irony, slapstick, or inspired irrelevance is unrewarding. They either 'get' you, or you remain stonily silent. To me, the Frog Footman's casual estimate as to how long he proposes to sit outside the Duchess' house is inimitable. But once one begins to anatomize it, the savour is lost.

So, likewise, with other forms of comic humour, unrelated to the gentle wit of Lewis Carroll, and by no means necessarily related to one another. Even a quick survey of the best of the Victorian 'comics' immediately shows that the real test is that of individuality. It would indeed be a tyro who would confuse the humour of *Punch* with the humour of *Fun*, or of *Judy*, or of one or two others. In alluding to *Judy*, one means the original Victorian *Judy* (1867–1907) long since defunct, no reference being made to a more recent periodical of similar title.

To say much about *Punch*, born in 1841 and still flourishing, would be supererogatory. Everyone knows it, or of it; it has its own historians in Marion H. Spielmann and, more recently, R. G. G. Price. Its mountainous files have been ransacked by authors and journalists galore, and by students of social and political history. No other humorous paper has ever enlisted such a galaxy of the famous – and famous-to-be – in art and literature, from John Leech and Tenniel, to Charles Keene and du Maurier, Linley Sambourne, Phil May, and Harry Furniss; from Thackeray, Thomas Hood, Albert Smith, Douglas Jerrold, to Burnand and 'F. Anstey'. I speak wholly of a past which, despite having been excavated with an almost scientific thoroughness, remains as exalted as ever.

Even so, in our search of Victorian corners, there may be a detail or so which, if by no means unknown, is worth singling out for discussion. Take the case of John Tenniel (1820–1914), not knighted till 1893.

Tenniel's position is unique. He remains the Olympian Jove of cartoonists. His conceptions were as classically impressive as were his superb powers of composition and draughtsmanship. When one recalls that this great artist in black-and-white lost the sight of an eye in a fencing mishap, one's respect for his genius is multiplied. The same hand which gave us such world-famed cartoons as the prophetic *The Shadow in the Path*, the *Dropping the Pilot*, or, in lighter though none the less impressive vein, *The Political Mrs Gummidge*, had also captured the fleeting light and shade of Carroll's *Alice* books. Tenniel was *Punch's* Blind Homer.

George du Maurier, too, lost the sight of an eye. It was in 1859, and the remaining eye failed in 1891–2, but happily recovered its sight. It was partly with the purpose of resting it that du Maurier started on fiction. His spasm of blindness was one of the causes of *Trilby*.

2

A commentator once wrote of George Louis Palmella Busson du Maurier (1831–96) that his art was 'vulgar'. I cannot imagine what was meant by this, unless the writer was confusing the satirizing of vulgarity with vulgar performance. In fact, George du Maurier was an unusually skilled and perceptive draughtsman who perfectly mirrored the aristocratic and upper middle-class tone of his day. His jokes tell the tale of 'Society', whether hallmarked or merely pretentious. His inimitable dukes and duchesses may have withered, but, in other garb, his vulgarians and climbers remain. 'Sir Gorgius Midas' is still in our midst, and so, perchance less attractively, is 'Mrs Ponsonby de Tomkyns'.

Like Keene's, du Maurier's humour, where it distorts at all, distorts very slightly and subtly his *monde*; but his satire is none the less pungent for lacking a farcical basis. It is witty; but when, rarely enough, he indulged in sheer fantasy it could shock like a nightmare.

Though du Maurier's preoccupation with the upper crust did not exclude sympathetic comment on the lower classes (as they were called), nobody understood better than Charles Keene (1823–91) the traits of the middle class downwards. To a considerable extent, his types were drawn from professional folk or tradesmen, and his characterization is rich. Neither malicious nor frivolous, it touches very near truth. His are actual flesh-and-blood types; one might meet them any day in the street, the fields, or beside a Highland loch without more than casually thinking that their dress was old-fashioned. His creations exist in a true time dimension. Their Present has a Past and a Future. And when one has said all these things, let us rejoice in Charles Keene's admirable draughtsmanship, rendered with a sensitivity of touch which did not always survive its translation to wood-engraving.

It was Edward Linley Sambourne (1844–1910) who succeeded Tenniel as *Punch's* chief cartoonist at the turn of the century. The two men's styles were utterly different. Where Tenniel's was epic, Sambourne's was lyric, but he too was an admirable draughtsman, gifted with fancy, fecund ingenuity, an elegant prankishness quite medieval. He would caricature a great man with the fittest of comical attributes; he would portray a gleaming-limbed nymph and surround her with creeping grotesques. Whether detailed or simple, his work – one looks back to his heyday – is masterly. When he took over from Tenniel, he was past his prime. Many years ago, I rescued the 'original' of one of his late *Punch* cartoons from the shilling box outside a secondhand bookseller's; it was unimportant. One judges an artist by his best, and, on this basis, Sambourne is a vivid pictorial poet. If his technique sometimes lacks contrast, in vision and grace of ideas it stands in its own sphere unrivalled. And Sambourne's illustrations to the 1889 edition of Kingsley's *The Water Babies* are to the magic tale of the little chimney-sweep what Tenniel's drawings are to Carroll's *Alice*. 'How he, our comrade, with his pencil lent your fancy's speech a firmer spell', as Sir Owen Seaman phrased it in *Punch* when Carroll died.

A noteworthy photograph of Tenniel and Sambourne together was reproduced by 'Peter-

Fig 34. Mivvins who doesn't 'take' well, being posed in a photographer's studio. 'Enery, bring the 'Ead-Rest!' A typical Charles Keene 'cut' from *Punch*, 7th June, 1873. *(By permission)*

borough' of the *Daily Telegraph* on March 14, 1960, a few months before HRH The Princess Margaret's marriage to Sambourne's great-grandson, now the Earl of Snowdon. The photograph of two elderly gentlemen urbanely toasting each other is interesting in its own right as portraiture, and because it was taken by Sambourne himself, using remote control. In the sunburst of comments on a royal occasion, 'Peterborough's' find was of singular value.

3

Harry Furniss (1854–1925) had also illustrated Carroll – the two *Sylvie and Bruno* books (1889 and '93) in which his aboundingly facile line found rather more than freedom of action. There was an hilarious quality in Furniss's art; nothing quite like it had been seen in *Punch* before his arrival there in 1880. He laughed and slashed, soothed and slashed again; and not in *Punch* alone. A doughty opponent of the Royal Academy, Furniss attacked that already venerable body in *Harry Furniss's Royal Academy: An Artistic Joke* (1887), and again in *Royal Academy Antics* (1890). A more vitriolic onslaught than the latter could scarcely be found. Even Royal Academy exhibitors were known to have a copy on their shelves.

Furniss's illustrations to Dickens and Thackeray (1910 and '11) are beyond our present scope. By then, the creator of the 'Since then I have used no other' jest, and who had dashingly decorated the *Essence of Parliament* feature, had long since parted brass rags with *Punch*. In 1894, he launched his own humorous weekly, its ill-advised name *Lika Joko* which he had himself used as an occasional pseudonym in *Punch*. It was not a success.

4

Furniss was not the sole artist to fall out with Burnand. Another was James F. Sullivan, who should not be confused (as he has been) with Edmund J. Sullivan, adept in a different branch of black-and-white. James F. Sullivan, who sometimes signed himself 'Jassef' (for Jas. F.), died in 1936, aged 83, having long since retired. His sojourn with *Punch* was a brief episode in a career in which he had won distinction. His name was made on *Fun*, the 'penny *Punch*' as it was known in its heyday; 'that really comic "comic" paper', to quote a much later epithet by one of its former staff-writers.[31]

In its great period, *Fun* was owned by those famous wood-engravers the Brothers Dalziel, George (1815–1903) and Edward (1817–1905). They extended their scope, became magazine owners and, of course, made their own blocks. It was in 1870 that they took over *Fun*. For the previous five years Edward Wylam had owned it; then he purchased the patent of a renowned brand of dog biscuits.

Fun cost the Dalziels £6,000. They found it a valuable property. If *Punch* has its own roll of honour, so too had *Fun* before and after the Dalziel *régime*. That finely sensitive artist G. J. Pinwell; Frederick Barnard and James Mahoney, both very prominent in the second wave of Dickens's illustrators; Henry Doyle, younger brother of the 'Dicky' Doyle who designed what for so long remained the *Punch* cover; Hubert Herkomer, later knight and a 'von', and one of the most distinguished RA's of his time; also Ernest Griset, the draughtsman whose animal grotesques won renown. Such and Sullivan too – we shall come to him later – were some of *Fun's* illustrators. And among other contributors at this time or that were W. S. Gilbert in his *avatar* as 'Bab', Austin Dobson, George R. Sims, George Manville Fenn, Clement Scott, George Augustus Sala, and 'Arthur Sketchley', creator of the popular 'Mrs Brown' series: a feature on Sairey Gamp lines.

When the Dalziels took over, Tom Hood was editor, son of the author of *The Song of the Shirt* (1843), that moving and great-hearted poem which must always be one of the jewels in *Punch's* crown. Tom Hood the younger had talent of his own; his death in 1874 was a loss. His immediate successor, Henry Sampson, later founded *The Referee* (1877) and left *Fun* soon afterwards, taking with him Henry Chance Newton, who became 'Carados' to Sampson's 'Pendragon'. Richard Butler came next in *Fun's* editorial succession;[32] but let us discuss 'Jassef' Sullivan.

5

According to the Brothers Dalziel, James F. Sullivan was 'a student at South Kensington when he first forwarded sketches for our inspection; . . . . we at once availed ourselves of his

[31] H. Chance Newton: *Cues and Curtain Calls* (John Lane, 1927), pp. 26–7.
[32] *Op. cit.*

drawings'.[33] Enough has been said to establish that *Fun* was no rag. Enrolment on its staff was an asset to any young artist, but, as time went by, Sullivan became an asset to *Fun*, drawing, writing and versifying. He also worked for *Tom Hood's Comic Annual*, issued from the *Fun* office and another of the Dalziels' possessions. In the *Strand Magazine*, Sullivan's feature *The Queer Side of Things* attracted attention; and in 1896, the first volume of *Pearson's Magazine* presented *The Great Water Joke*, a typical exercise in Sullivan's satirical wit, which lost nothing by its mock ingenuousness.

> 'I'm sorry!' said the Company; 'I'm perfectly distraught
> To think you haven't water, but it happens there's a drought.
> I'm sorry!' said the Company; 'my grief is very great:
> The Winter's frozen up the mains; but kindly pay the rate.'

Sullivan's brief connexion with *Punch* has been glanced at already; but his self-illustrated books of short stories, *Here They Are!* and *Here They Are Again!*, both published in the 1890s, are worth noting for their embodiment of typically Sullivanesque fancies. In *Here They Are Again!*, for example, we are indulged with a tale of a good dragon who roamed

Fig. 35. 'And this is the Author's brutal and overbearing vanity . . .', by 'Jassef' Sullivan, detail from *The British Working Man.* (1878)

around destroying naughty knight-errants. In private life, 'Jassef' was a keen and discriminating antiquary, with a feeling for arms and armours, and a background of old oak. Though, of his own choice, his career as a humorist had been abandoned long before his death in 1936, Sullivan's name remained known to the last in such circles as the Meyrick Society, that exclusive assembly of *amateurs d'armes*.

6

'In the comic paper called *Fun*, the admirable artist of that journal, Mr Sullivan, laid hold of my puppets, and made them play a different game', wrote Frith of his own 'series of five

[33] *The Brothers Dalziel: A Record* (Methuen, 1901), p. 312.

pictures representing the career of a fraudulent financier. . . .'[34] Such a theme was right up Sullivan's street.

As a draughtsman, he was almost always at his best in a grotesque vein. Attempts to be 'serious' seemed, on the whole, to defeat him. He revelled in the sheerest of farce and was not infrequently scathing. For sheer monumental absurdity, his whimsies are unsurpassed in their sphere. He had all a true cartoonist's justness in poking shrewd nonsense at life.

My impression is that, for many years, Sullivan worked without models, in some cases basing his characters' facial contortions on his own reflection in a mirror. (In this he would not have been alone among artists, and Dickens himself is credited with similar antics). Admittedly Sullivan's *method* developed, but his *style* was early apparent. It was, I should think, in the 1890s that his method attained maximum fullness, perhaps due in part to an occasional use of models.

But if Sullivan's penwork became more elaborate, his humour remained as it had been, nor does it follow that his more highly wrought drawings are the funniest. For my part, I doubt whether Sullivan was ever quite at home in the *Punch* of his period.

7

'Jassef' Sullivan worked for *Fun* for some twenty years. Though his views often diverged from editorial policy, he maintained independence. *Fun*'s politics were more advanced than *Punch's* liberalism; its 'big cuts' had a decidedly radical complexion.

Sullivan cared nothing for this. He satirized anyone he chose: on the one hand complacent officialdom and vested interests; on the other, the more brainless type of workman or china-smashing skivvy. Stupidity was, to him, a vice. He hated all forms of officiousness, made no allowance for causes, but neither had he any favourites.

Probably his best-known series is *The British Working Man. By One who does not believe in him*, which appeared first in *Fun* and was later reissued in book form from the *Fun* Office in Fleet Street. It aroused mirth and resentment in equal proportions. Not that 'Jassef' cared a jot at the time, though later, and for whatever reason, he was said to have taken a dislike to the book, bought up all copies he could find of it and burned the lot.[35] This could be one of the reasons why *The British Working Man* is now in short supply. That Sullivan's temper in it is frequently couched in terms of an almost passionate resentment, often with justification if scarcely stopping at savagery, does not stay it from being very funny indeed.

8

A selection of Sullivan's colleagues on *Fun* and *Hood's Comic Annual* – distinct from *old* Tom Hood's *Comic Annual* – awaits mention. First, I summon up George Gordon Fraser, a clever exponent of pictorial slapstick. If his method was wordy, his drawings were instinct with a humour which, now and again, became weird. He was skilled in presenting a bizarre form of practical joke with, in one of its phases, an oddly nightmarish quality.

[34] *The Race for Wealth.* Frith: *op. cit.*, p. 358.
[35] Private Information.

That phase strikes home grimly in the after-light of his tragic death. It is as though his imps and bogies revolted, screaming with glee. In the hard winter of 1895 Gordon Fraser went skating in Huntingdonshire. His body was taken from under the ice.

Fraser had an interesting foible: a leaning to Jacobitism crops up now and then in his comedy. One looks back again at a surname with notable Jacobite connexions.

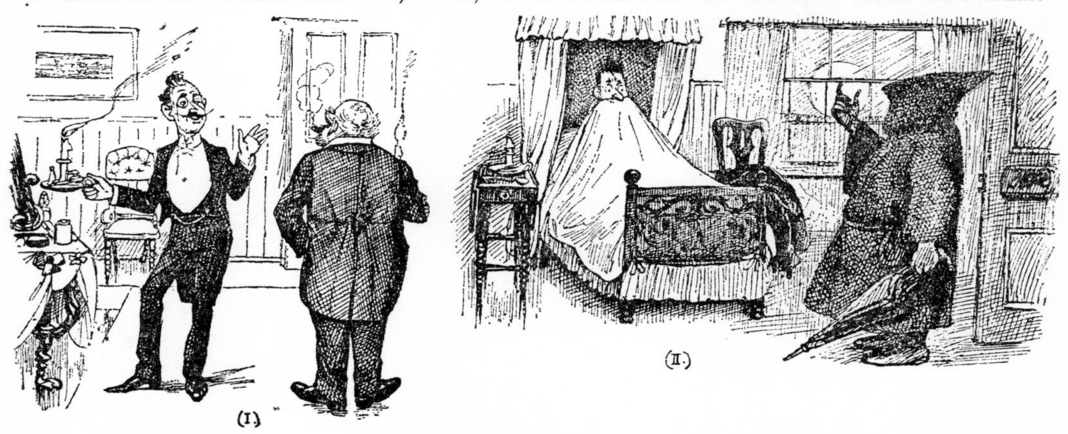

Fig. 36. The guest who didn't believe in ghosts. Note dado, draped dressing-table, and a (perhaps) antique bedside chair. Detail from Charles Gordon Fraser sequence in *Hood's Comic Annual*, 1894.

John William Houghton[36] had no such romantic enthusiasms. His humour can be simply described as honest to God. 'Jack' Houghton (or 'Johnnie' as Sullivan called him) was an amusing and competent draughtsman in his own right. Like 'Jassef', he drew, wrote and rhymed. In *Tom Hood's Comic Annual* for 1890, there is an excellent example of his skill in a burlesque of Ibsen's *Ghosts*, which he called *Bogies: A Drama in Three Acts, Written in Ibsens of Mind by Schottata FFrog, Esq.* I recall the mystification with which I, when a child, read this satire, wondering why on earth LONA should find OSWALD crouched in a chair, exhibiting such hereditary stigmata as a black eye, one cork and one wooden leg; being furthermore armless on one side, partly fingerless on the other, missing an ear, and branded on the forehead.

I met Houghton once in his old age, long since retired from the work which had left him high and dry. And, in the Arts Club, my Father made me known to an elderly red-faced man with a dark moustache and a loud voice, Gordon Thomson who, long ago, had been *Fun's* political cartoonist.

Thomson was at his merriest outside the political arena, as when guying the Royal Academy. In his *Fun's Academy Skits* he rivalled Furniss. Even the great Sir John Gilbert commended his skill in this field. Houghton wrote the rhymes to Thomson's *Academy Skits*. Were at least some of the typically Victorian puns also his, it would not be surprising. As for instance (and

[36] Distinct from Arthur Boyd Houghton (1836–1875), an Associate of the Old Society, and despite semi-blindness a celebrated illustrator; also, at one time, with the Dalziels.

Fig. 37. The Waggish Witch. Details from a bizarre sequence by Charles Gordon Fraser in *Hood's Comic Annual* for 1894, recalling a motif by Gustave Doré.

Fig. 38. Scene from *Bogies*, John W. Houghton's forgotten skit on *Henrik* Ibsen's *Ghosts* in *Hood's Comic Annual*, 1890.

whoever their perpetrator) the following gems from *Fun's Academy Skits*, as published in book form, 1882.

Of a landscape by George Adolphus ('Dolly') Storey, *Coracles on the Dee – Llantysilio*, we read:

'794. – Coracles on the Dee – Verysillyo', with the comment 'You will see that the coracles are most coracley drawn'.

What G. A. Storey, better-known as a figure and portrait painter, had to say to this is unknown. Nor is it on record how that admired landscape painter Ernest Parton, whose *Waning of the Year* had been bought by the Chantrey in 1879, reacted to Gordon Thomson's treatment of him in 1882. Parton ran a strong line in crepuscular effects, so the '82 *Skit* showed an oblong enclosing an unrelieved fog without any detail whatever. Beneath was the caption:

'723. – Twilight; or, the Parton Day. Ernest Parton.'

Fig. 39. At the Academy, Susie is trotting her uncle from Canada round the picture Galleries. A typical John W. Houghton drawing from *Fun* (1887).

9

It was, I believe, that notable water-colour painter and illustrator Charles Green, himself a cousin of the younger Tom Hood, who gave my father an introduction to *Fun* and *Hood's Comic Annual.* Fred Roe began drawing for *Fun* in 1890, by when he was already known as an historical and *genre* painter.

Roe's comic 'stuff' was done 'on top' of his figure painting. He set aside each Thursday evening for it, and laboured well into the murk. *Fun*, *Judy*, *Ally Sloper's Half-Holiday*, and *Larks* (the last a minor Dalziel presentation which, I think, did not last) were among his engagements. In the long run, five or six periodicals were carrying his work.

Fun had changed hands in 1893, but Sullivan had left before them, and Roe had taken over his centre-page feature, facing Gordon Thomson's political cartoon. Not that Roe's manner owed anything to 'Jassef's'. It was more concerned with externals, and, though revelling in comic characterization, had no hornet-like sting. His was essentially good-humoured, rather boisterous mirth in fluent black-and-white line.

But things were not well with the paper. Editorial policy changed, and resignations followed, Fred Roe's among them. He had other openings in pictorial journalism, and maintained some of them for a while; but so much late work was productive of eye-strain, and there was, too, the question as to whether what had been a side-line was threatening to take charge at the expense of his paint. So a day came when the comic grind was abandoned, though, to the end of his long life, the artist would draw 'Shikees' (as he called them) for his own pleasure and that of his circle.

10

Roe's work for *Judy* was never extensive. I doubt if he quite *felt* that paper after its character changed. The Dalziels acquired it in 1872 and held it till 1888.[37] Then Gilbert Dalziel (who

[37] *The Brothers Dalziel*, pp. 318–28.

had studied at the Slade under Poynter) took it over, introducing all manner of improvements. The tone was raised, the old robustious humour was dropped. The general effect was to make *Judy* a counterpart of *Punch*. In came Bernard Partridge, Frederick Pegram, Raven-Hill, F. H. Townsend, all since famous on *Punch*. In came Fred Barnard and W. G. Baxter, and Maurice Greiffenhagen (not yet RA). Greiffenhagen worked also for *Tom Hood's Comic Annual*. Though an illustrator of note, he was somewhat miscast as a humorist.

Now, Gilbert Dalziel was a very shrewd man, who could make a success of a paper; but in 'refining' *Judy* he opened the door to academic humour and the illustrated joke. Before the changeover, *Judy* was strongly individual. It was droll. So let us retrace our steps to the 1870s and '80s, when Charles H. Ross was in the editorial chair; and Ross had a sense of sheer fun. His writings revel in purposeful anticlimax. But let us consider one of Ross's most memorable illustrators, the lady who signed herself 'Marie Duval'.

II

Ross, wrote the Brothers Dalziel,[38]

'was also a skilful draughtsman, and we engraved hundreds of his drawings. His pages of humorous pictures, which appeared in Judy, were generally signed 'Marie Duval' (his wife's maiden name), and the subjects often savoured somewhat of French origin.'

The last words presumably allude to style rather than to content, and are not a Victorian synonym for riskiness (than which nothing could be further from the fact).

Even so, it cannot pass unchallenged. 'Marie Duval' is a traceable person. She figures in *Thieme-Becker* (which has nothing to say of Charles H. Ross), and, more importantly, in the second volume of Ellen Clayton's *English Female Artists* (1876).[39] As a contemporary account by one of Marie's colleagues on *Judy*, this is noteworthy. Of *Judy* itself, Clayton writes: 'It is a little remarkable that this journal employs the services of three of the four ladies who draw humorous subjects', *i.e.* Marie Duval, Adelaide Claxton, and Ellen Clayton herself.

Putting our material together, and quoting when needful, we reach the following details of Marie Duval. Her parents were French, her maiden name was Isabelle Émilie de Tessier, and she was born in Paris in 1850. 'At the age of seventeen,' says Clayton,

'she was a governess, but quitted that laborious profession for the stage, and appeared at several London and provincial theatres. In 1874 she made a very successful tour through the country, playing various roles, among others "Jack Sheppard" – in which part she created surprise by the striking resemblance she bore to Mrs Keeley.'

It was while working Yarmouth in this part that Marie had a serious accident, which, though she carried on bravely as long as she could, brought the evening's show to a premature close. And from that catastrophe, Ellen Clayton passes on to Marie's illustrative career.

'Of all the comic artists now living, with the exception of Charles Keene and William Brunton, this lady is the only one who can be called really a humorous designer.' Though Clayton's selection is far too narrow, there is a basis of truth in her criticism. Marie Duval

[38] *Op. cit.*, p. 320.

[39] Published by Tinsley Brothers, II, p. 330 ff. Ellen (Eleanor) Creathorne Clayton, afterwards Needham, was the author's full name.

was essentially a *comic* artist. Self-taught in art, her drawings had little to commend them by the academic standards of the day. But funny they undoubtedly were, and far more so than many technically 'better' performances. We may perhaps reserve our opinion when Clayton goes on: 'Miss Duval is probably at her best in coloured subjects, as, for example, in a nursery book . . . . called *Queens and Kings, and other Things*, to which she contributed numerous grotesque subjects under the stately pseudonym of the "Princess of Hesse Schartzbourg".' Yet another pseudonym of hers was 'Noir', because she 'always' dressed in black.

What, then, is the answer to the Dalziels' assertion that Charles H. Ross was himself 'Marie Duval'? My guess – and it is no more than a guess – is that Ross passed his wife's account for drawings under his own name, thus simplifying book-keeping. He could then draw for *all* work by the Ross's and settle with madame in private. Such arrangements, by no means unknown, have been conducted in the strictest probity. Is it arguable that such a manœuvre by Mr and Mrs Ross might have confused the Dalziels, writing years afterwards, the more especially as Ross was himself a draughtsman? The curious will find some woodcuts from his designs in the British Museum Print Room. Most of them have affinities with 'Duval'.

12

Before quitting the subject of *Judy* as such, two other of its artists must be mentioned, one being none less than the greatest illustrator of Dickens and numerous other authors 'Phiz', otherwise Hablot Knight Browne, who died in 1882. His contributions to *Judy* (collected in

Fig. 40. 'Ga'long! you forward thing, you!' (*The Mermaid's Tale*) by Archibald Chasemore, from *Rattle-trap Rhymes and Tootletum Tales* [1876]. (*British Museum*)

book form as *A Shillingsworth of Phiz*), drawn with his left hand when health had deserted him, are pathetic shadows of greatness. But Archibald Chasemore, who had worked for *Punch* before going over to *Judy*, comes well within our orbit. His and Ross's *Rattletrap Rhymes* and *Tootletum Tales*[40] in *Judy* were clever and catchy, as was his illustrated series on *How Certain Places got their Names*, which, if lacking Carroll's touch, solemnly advanced

Fig. 41. 'Then said she, solemnly and slow, One single word, and that was "Bo" !' Chasemore in Stage Whispers

etymological nonsense worthy of the master himself. One mock-historical absurdity must serve as a sample. It purports to trace the origin of the 'Welsh Harp' at Hendon.

'Whilst the King was marching on to St Albans, hearing that the enemy were at hand, he ordered one of his generals to go first and cut the way through, single-handed; but the general complained that his sword, notched by former battles, was too blunt. "*Well sharp*-en it!" said the monarch. It is a curious fact that this incident took place where the "Welsh Harp" now stands, and no doubt the name of the inn is a corruption of his memorable words. – *History of Herts.*'

If one chooses to mispronounce Herts as 'Hurts', the joke is accented. Accompanying it was an equally incredible 'cut' of the anonymous King and equally anonymous 'general' in armours which would scarcely win Claude Blair's approval, the general dubiously displaying an enormous sword with a blade like an embryo hacksaw.

The strong literary element in Chasemore's humour – an element favoured in his time – should not deflect admiration of his drawings. Among other facets, they show a decided ability to render ladies of the chorus in a manner distinctly fetching, without ever transgressing good taste. The late Herbert Granville Fell recalled to me how, in his young days, he and his fellow art students would copy Chasemore's 'girls' for sheer joy of the skill with which they were executed.

[40] 'Collected' as '*by Ambrose Clarke and Charles H. Ross*' [1876].

13. The Gothic-cum-Norman Revival hits the cartoons. Gladstone and Morley superbly drawn as Macbeth and Seyton in Tenniel's 'big cut' for *Punch*, March 27, 1886. 'This push will cheer me ever, or disseat me now . . . Give me my armour.' (*Reproduced by permission*)

14. Du Maurier's art could have grim undertones as in this *Punch* drawing: 'Window Studies—A Quiet Pipe (In Remembrance of March, 1887)', published on April 2nd in that year

A 'Glastonbury' Chair in an illustration by (Sir) John Everett Millais for Harriet Martineau's *Sister Anna's Probation* in *Once a Week* (1862)

Chasemore's relation to *Judy* was not unlike Houghton's to *Fun*. His neat little drawings are technically able – and funny. In a way, they remind one of W. S. Gilbert's illustrations to his own early work *The Bab Ballads*. These delectable rhymes, later collected in book form (1869 and '73), were appearing at intervals in *Fun* from 1866–71. Their author was an occasional contributor to *Punch*; and that *Punch* did not get *The Bab Ballads* was due to an editorial error of judgment. *The Yarn of the 'Nancy Bell'* was submitted – and declined as being 'too cannibalistic'. . . .

SEVEN

Featuring 'Ally Sloper'

'. . . . with no more hair upon his head (which was a large one, and very shining) than there is upon an egg, ...' CHARLES DICKENS

I

CHARLES H. ROSS's *régime* on *Judy* had a result which outlived that paper itself. He and Marie Duval had, between them, created 'Ally Sloper', and it was Marie's crudely inimitable drawings which gave physical form to that immensely popular creature of comic fiction. The point is worth making in view of a mistaken belief that the type originated with *Ally Sloper's Half-Holiday*, whereas, when that comic was launched, Sloper had been for a long while in being.

According to H. Chance Newton, in *Cues and Curtain Calls* (John Lane, The Bodley Head, 1927), Ally Sloper 'was invented at the Surrey Theatre' by 'Marie Duval', at a time when Ross was concerned in the management of that house. Golden-haired 'Little Marie', the 'soubrette of the company', 'first drew' Sloper 'in connection with a penny almanac named after him'. Certainly *Ally Sloper's Comic Kalendar* had been put out by *Judy*, but that this was 'The Eminent's' first appearance is, to my mind, dubious. However, Chance Newton is doubtless right in stating that Ross got Marie 'to amplify the Ally Sloper idea, he himself taking on the writing of fresh libretto [*sic*], stories, jokes, etc., to carry the character out more fully'.

Ally Sloper was a Micawberesque figure, impecunious, pompous, mock-philosophical, in shabby, old-fashioned attire. Self-deceptively venal, he lacked the equipment to further his miserable little intrigues. In a state of foolish, kind-hearted dignity, he ever tried to carry off life in style, only to be thwarted, exposed, tripped up, and generally plunged in the liquid.

Fig. 42. Micawber as realised by Phiz for Dickens's *David Copperfield.* (1850). (*Detail*).

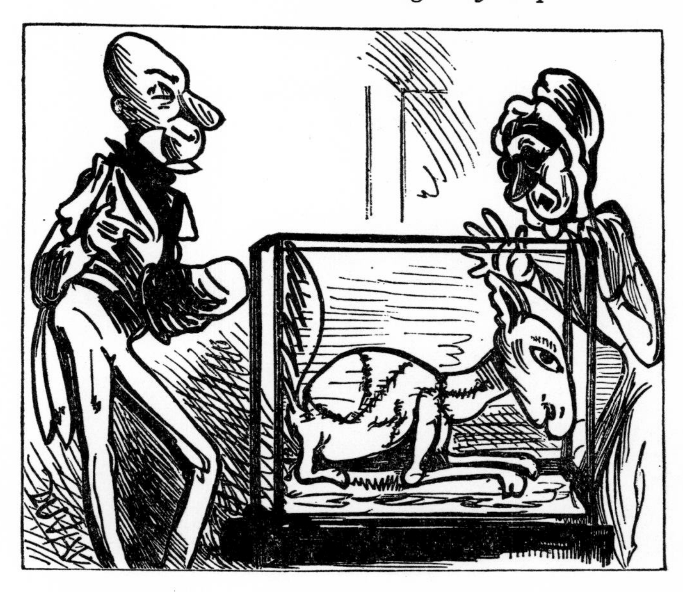

Fig. 43. Sloper fails as an 'eminent stuffist': the unrecognisable pet. By Marie Duval from *Ally Sloper's Book of Beauty* [1877]. (*British Museum*)

Nobody can study Ally Sloper for long without likening him to Phiz's realizations of Wilkins Micawber in *David Copperfield* (1850). Ellen Clayton (*op. cit.*) compared these two figures of fiction, but drew no inference from their general resemblance. But there were others who held that Ally Sloper had been in a measure suggested by Dickens's Mr Micawber. Whether or not this was so in fact – and Chance Newton ignores it – one might be forgiven for assuming some such derivation. Ally is a Micawber run badly to seed.

From a casual start, Ally Sloper became a stock feature of *Judy*. In Marie Duval's drawings and Ross's text, he and his friend Ikey Moses 'caught on'. Moses was the keen foil to the elderly, disreputable child that was Ally. Were Peter Pan to become an easy-going old man, lazy, boozy, with a bleary eye on the main chance, he might turn out something like the Duval-Ross Sloper. *Per contra*, the fictitious Moses was shrewd, alert, cunning, well able to take care of himself and of anything that came his way.

We have already seen that *Ally Sloper's Comic Kalendar* was a *Judy* by-product; so too were collected editions of the squalid Sloperian saga put out in paper-back form from the *Judy* office in Shoe Lane. These, though a good deal made up of *clichés* from *Judy* itself, are rewarding – when one can find them. Relevant titles were *Ally Sloper, Ally Sloper's Book of Beauty, Ally Sloper's Guide to Paris, Ally Sloper's Comic Crackers*, and *Ally Sloper's Journey*.

2

To give a taste of the original Sloper in what were presumably Charles H. Ross's own words – the style is his – extracts from two Sloperian whimsies in *Judy* tell more than pages of description. For example:

'Incidents of an unexpected nature have taken place in the career of A. SLOPER, the eminent *litterateur*. He has been snatched from the brink of that goal from which no traveller

SLOPER AT HOME.

[*The dear old man himself supplied the sketch for this picture—tears of love and paternal pride glistening in his eyes, as with simple pathos, he dwelt upon the details of the touching scene. How it is—if half the noble sentiments he uttered really came from his heart—*SLOPER *should recently have been summoned to the Police Court for neglecting to contribute to the support of Mrs. S., at present an inmate of St. Starvercum-bag-o'bones Workhouse,* JUDY'S *Office Boy regrets his inability to explain.*]

Fig. 44. Marie Duval's frontispiece to *Some Playful Episodes in the career of Ally Sloper* [1873], showing that Sloper, like Wilkins Micawber, had twins. (*British Museum*) returns, and trusts that the printer will take care how he manages the vowels, as it may make a serious difference to A. SLOPER's moral character.'

And again:

'Mr Whatshisname, the wellknown and worthy magistrate, having had A. SLOPER's card, invited him to enter, and held out his hand, in which A. SLOPER placed his hat and umbrella, and took his seat by Mr Whatshisname on the bench. A brief interval then ensued, in which A. SLOPER was forcibly removed from the Court, and his hat and umbrella thrown after him. The first case was then called on . . . .'

One would like to know why the Ross faction chose Sloper, a surname with honourable connexions in real life, for their fictitious 'Ally'?

3

By the time that *Judy's* style changed to a staider and more *Punch*-like character, Sloper was already an established success. *Judy* became Sloperless. Ross (says Chance Newton)[41] 'sold the idea of Ally Sloper' to Gilbert Dalziel (son of Edward and nephew of George Dalziel) who remodelled *Judy* and gave Ally a paper of his own. This, *Ally Sloper's Half-Holiday*, was launched in 1884, and became a popular success. I have heard it said that it brought in Gilbert Dalziel £30,000; but that is as may be.

Fig. 45. Ally Sloper with Snatcher: late Victorian Door-porter. (*Mr and Mrs Michael Maynard*)

[41] H. Chance Newton: *op. cit.*, page 274

At first, some old 'Duval' blocks were re-used in the *Half-Holiday*, but many new features were introduced and Sloper's image was revivified by the paper's chief cartoonist, W. G. Baxter. A skilful draughtsman with a firm fluent line, Baxter was altogether more technically equipped than Marie Duval. He took over her Sloperian conventions: Ally's old-fashioned clothes and dropsical hat, the battered old cabbage-gamp, the bald head, general aspect; but, in the long run he burlesqued a burlesque. Set side by side, his Sloper differs in detail and spirit from Marie's. Where hers was seedy, his was grotesque. The celebrated nose became pathologically bulbous; the lean legs in tight trousers with straps – an amazing hangover of costume – degenerated into mere sticks with bloated boots at their ends. Yet this was the image which so impressed itself on a later generation of Sloperians that many, who can still recall the *Half-Holiday*, accept it as that of the one and only Eminent. Moreover, Christmas cards, metal door-stops, tobacco-pipes, pottery jugs and children's dolls all helped to indoctrinate an avid public with the Sloperian epistle according to W. G. Baxter – and, of course, Gilbert Dalziel. To the masses, Ally Sloper, the 'urban John Bull' as Wells oddly styled him in *Tono-Bungay* (1909), was as familiar a figure as, say, Mickey Mouse or Pinky and Perky were to be to later generations.

In the *Half-Holiday*, too, more play was made with Ally's 'family'. Doubtless in view of prejudice in certain quarters, Moses was dropped; but Mrs Sloper, her fetching daughter Tootsie, Aunt Geezer, and Snatcher the dog, among others, made up a household to which Tootsie's girl friend, the fascinatingly named Lardi Longsox, was a happy addition. (Whether or not the 'Lardi' part of it was based on the name – nothing more – of that colourful Victorian stage-personality, Lardy Wilson, is beyond my knowledge.)

Fig. 46. Sloper as re-originated by W. G. Baxter, and here drawn by Archibald Chasemore.

W. G. Baxter's Sloperian vein is seen at its best in the 'Sloper Award of Merit': a comic diploma conferring the letters FOS on its recipients. FOS may look a little like FRS, but it means 'Friend of Sloper', and people in many different walks of life were tickled to receive the Freedom of the Sloperies. It was rumoured that even Queen Victoria herself was entitled to add FOS to her other distinctions, had such been the Royal pleasure. One speculates, as to whether Her Majesty was in this instance amused?

The Sloper Award of Merit was issued, hand-coloured, and bearing a great waxen seal, impressed with a device of the famous hat in rays of glory, surrounded by the legend '*ALLY SLOPER FRIEND OF MAN* ID ON THE BOTTLE.' Scenes from the life of A. Sloper from birth – well back in the eighteenth century, judging by details of dress – and throughout his career, culminating in an apotheosis with a red-headed FAME PRESIDING OVER A. SLOPER, flank a pompously phrased certification. A huge and splashing 'signature' completes the effect.

It is a pity that, in after years, this decisive, dexterous, diverting Diploma should have been replaced by one less notable.

EIGHT

Aspects of 'Do-It-Yourself'

'We continue our directions . . . . , which our pupils will now find divested, we trust, of every difficulty.' THE FAMILY FRIEND

I

FROM comics to children's toys is an easy transition. The general aim of this chapter is to poke around for Victorian equivalents of what is now known as 'Do-it-Yourself', but as toys have been mentioned, let us begin with them.

Not all kinds of toys; but such as Ebenezer Landells (1808–60), a pupil of Bewick and himself a well-known wood engraver and one of the founders of *Punch*, discussed in his series of books on toy-making. Included in Landells' Popular Instructive Works were *The Boy's Own Toy-maker*, *The Girl's Own Toy-maker*, and *The Illustrative Paper Model Maker*: all published by Griffith and Farran, successors to Newbery and Harris – familiar names to collectors of *juvenilia*. Not that these books exhausted the sources of reference for the young person in search of reasonable occupation. There were others, besides which magazines were often ready to publish illustrated articles on 'How-to-do-it'. For the moment, however, it serves to focus on *The Girl's Own Toy-maker, and Book of Recreation*, originally published in 1860, and of which I have a copy of the fifth edition (1868). In this, the author (whose Introduction is baronially signed 'Landells' *tout court*) had as collaborator his daughter Alice Landells, which, in view of certain feminine mysteries revealed, was just as well. Nor was this entirely a matter of being 'quite nice'. Most male authors might be a shade chary of technicalities if 'How to dress a Doll' were the subject. And, in this instance, the doll is decidedly feminine. Not only are her frock and her hat, her cape and her pinafore, examined in detail, but such recondite matters as her flannel petticoat, hoop petticoat, white petticoat, and 'petticoat body', even her drawers and her night dress are displayed to public view, with full instruction on 'how-to-do-it'.

Fig. 47. 'Take a piece of calico . . .' Pattern for Doll's Drawers, from *The Girl's Own Toy-maker* (1860)

Clearly dolls so dressed were *lady* dolls, with a seemly amount of things that go underneath, and which *could* be mentioned because they were only dolls, weren't they. One feels, all the same, that *The Girl's Own Toy-maker's* public need not have been utterly amateur. That sad little figure in *Our Mutual Friend*, Jenny Wren, 'doll's dressmaker and manufacturer of ornamental pincushions and pen-wipers', was too expertly professional to need such advice; but there may well have been others, poor ladies and seamstresses, who felt that even an outlay of a half-crown on a book of this kind, with 'UPWARDS OF TWO HUNDRED ENGRAVINGS', might be a worth-while investment.

2

Pen-wipers, pincushions, needle-books, fans and hand-screens, watch-pockets and (decorative) fly-catchers all find place in the Landells' pages; and space is devoted to the making of toys of paper and cardboard. Dolls'-house furniture (cut out of cardboard) embraced such things as armchairs, couches, wash-hand stands, bedsteads and bed-steps. One could (if one

Fig. 48. From Victorian work-boxes: (*L–R*) Needle-book with vegetable-ivory covers; Knitted 'Strawberry' Needle-cleaner; Jockey-cap Pincushion, still studded with Victorian pins (*Mrs M. Maynard*).

Fig. 49. Fate Lady: fortune-telling toy from *The Girl's Own Toy-maker.*

chose) fashion a perambulator, a model cottage (recommended as 'a very neat embellishment for the drawing-room'), or a 'Fate Lady': the last being a fairy-like figure poised on a disc of pasteboard marked out with such enlightening 'fortunes' as:

> 'The fairy lady seals your doom,
> In that blest spot – your own kind home.'

or, more daringly:

> 'Nay, wise one, never look demure;
> You're not too modest, I am sure.'

And when such excitement palled, one could go on to the creation of Moss Baskets (covered in dried mosses or even unravelled worsted), Allspice Baskets (strung with allspice berries soaked in brandy to soften them), Alum Baskets (their frames coated with a solution of alum crystals), and Feather Baskets (which, happily, explain themselves). If all these, and not least the allspice variety, were fun to make, any scarcity of surviving examples can be borne with resignation.

Techniques have their own fascination, though I confess a lack of enthusiasm where the rather messy manufacture of alum baskets is concerned; but when it comes to the manufacture of hair-jewellery and the like, anyone may marvel at the sheer skill and patience involved. At which point, we take leave of the Landells in their Victorian corner; and pick up a magazine called *The Family Friend*: one of the periodicals catering for the womankind of the 1850s. Herein (New Series, Vol V) an inquiring reader is promptly stunned by full instructions as to how to make hair bracelets; to say nothing of hair-watch-guards, hair-rings, and decorative hair-nets (for the hair). 'Prepare thirty-two strands of twenty-four hairs each . . . . and arrange them on the table in eight groups of four', bearing in mind that 'twenty or thirty-inch hair is requisite' for the bracelet concerned, is the sort of thing that sends uninitiates

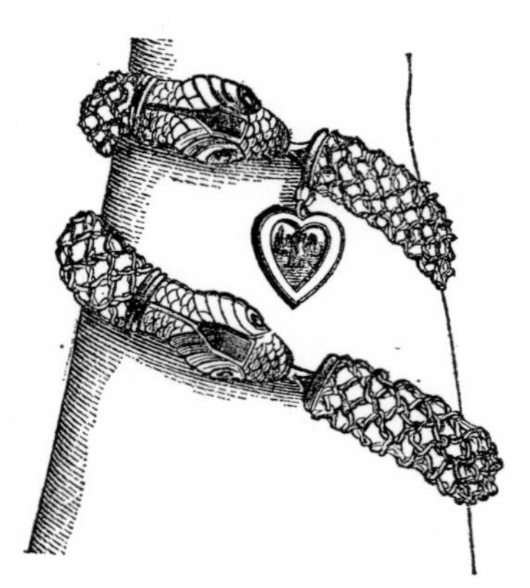

Fig. 50. Hair Bracelet. Woodcut from *The Family Friend,* Vol V. (1853)

scuttling to cover. To follow the process from start to finish is beyond my patience, to say nothing of my friend the reader's. However, we come to our senses again with the words: 'A serpent's or bird's head with jewelled eyes, forms a pretty finish; but [adds *The Family Friend* judicially] this is of course a matter of taste.'

Talking of Taste incites one to examine that peculiar form of it which resulted in the painting of ordinary window-panes in a manner distantly suggestive of actual stained glass. That such ornament could be usefully employed to mask unsightly outlooks, goes without saying. To claim that the basic idea was Victorian is excessive, though it was with the Victorian age that it reached its full flowering. It is, in effect, an extension of the notion of giving windows surrounds of ruby, deep blue, or amber glass, perhaps with cut stars in the corners, which carried through well after Regency times. And to confuse the merely painted window with true leaded lights (occasionally found in the shape of detachable dwarf blinds) portraying birds and flowers, or Burne-Jonesey maidens wilting over antique and unplayable musical instruments, would be deviationist. Some of these are not without merit, and, as they grow scarcer, may well recover a place in the aesthetic sun. Which is more than could be said for the average Victorian imitation stained glass, bought by the roll or the sheet, and displaying romantic figures in *lanzknecht* dress, gloomily suggestive of Germany in the early part of the sixteenth century. Such transparencies, stuck on to windows of even more depressing aspect, were not rendered gayer when, by unskilful application, they were left creased and bubbled. I speak entirely of the past; but when one has encountered surviving examples of this usage, of unmistakably Victorian vintage, the emotion induced has been one of the profoundest melancholy.

All of which has nothing to do with the oddly fascinating Lithophane panels, whether English or Continental, which, framed and hanging within a window or even used in lamps or candle-shades, are now collector's pieces. If, on average, their translucent porcellaneous attraction is more crafty than arty, they have a place in the evocation of later nineteenth-century interiors, not omitting, in the case of appropriate subjects, the clerical study.

No, it is what *The Family Friend* described as 'TRANSPARENT GLASS-PAINTING FOR WINDOWS, &c.' to which we have been working our way through a thicket of paragraphs. For this was 'a drawing-room occupation well worthy of . . . . attention and study': an occupation in which even ladies might indulge without detriment.

Fig. 51. Convolvulus pattern for window-painting (from *The Family Friend*). Cp 'Jassef' Sullivan's drawing (Fig. 52)

Fig. 52. 'And that unhappy Jane went up.' A typical mid-Victorian staircase as seen by 'Jassef' Sullivan. From *The British Working Man* (*Fun* Office, 1878) (cp. Fig. 50)

3

Up to a point, the method resembled one used in making real stained glass. A cartoon was drawn to the actual size of the panes.

'The pattern should be something bold and artistic; a scroll; any variety of star, or style of diamond or lattice-work; or groups of vine-leaves and grapes, or oak-leaves and acorns; or mottoes or initials in old English letters.'

(Again one detects a 'baronial' touch).

On the cartoon was laid a pane of ground glass, rough side uppermost, and on this were traced the outlines of the design 'with a fine camel-hair pencil [i.e. brush], moistened in copal varnish'. The glass was then moved to a sheet of unmarked paper, and painting done on it direct. There are other technicalities: details of cake-watercolours, varnishing, drying, and a final setting by immersion in 'clear cold spring water for five or ten minutes'; but these my reader is spared. What is more to our purpose as demonstrating an aspect of Victorian 'Do-it-Yourself' is the encouraging comment:

'Any person could prepare such a window as this, no knowledge of painting or drawing being requisite; all that is needful is a certain power of adaptation and combination, and some taste.'

'But most artistic effects may be produced, beautiful birds or butterflies, pleasant landscapes, groups of flowers, or of figures, animals, portraits; in short, any thing the skill of an artist could delineate on canvas, paper, or ivory, may be produced on glass, and with beautiful effect, if the lights and shades are carefully studied, bearing in mind that it is a transparent, and not a surface picture we would produce.'

4

A sister technique was that called Illuminated Glass-Painting, 'applicable to numberless ornamental articles; as letter-cases, blotting-books, portfolios, the lids of work or netting boxes, chess-tables, card-baskets, finger-plates, &c. &c.' This involved underpainted glass panels, as in the case of an aspiringly 'baronial' illuminated chess-table, each of its white squares bedight with a shield-of-arms, each black one with a formal pattern. If one had a coat-of-arms in the family, this was a pleasingly tactful way of displaying one's connexions. If one lacked such insignia, an heraldic engraver could soon turn up something; or arms of universities, colleges, schools might be pressed into service. Whatever the College of Arms might say, there was always a way out, even if, as a last resort, one made up arms out of one's head, which is less of an anatomical oddity than it sounds. What with gilding and silvering, colour and 'sparkle', the *ensemble* was brave.

So, too, with such things as screens and writing-desks. A pattern for a desk with bird-and-floral ornament is illustrated here (Fig 53). With due allowance for a stiff little woodcut of the 1850s, one feels that it makes the 'Why is a raven like a writing-desk?' riddle still harder to answer.

Fig. 53. Pattern of Writing-desk, enriched with illuminated Glass-painting. (From *The Family Friend*)

5

One of various curiosities in the International Exhibition of 1862 was a Frame and Trophy designed and executed by William Combe Sanders, of London. At first glance, this looked like a very delicate wood-carving, but it was in fact made of carved sheepskin. As such, it was a fine example of a kind of performance which appealed to Victorians as much by its sheer technical skill as by aesthetic excellence. Certainly, Mr Sanders's offering was very well done and, in its own way, enticing.

Decorative leather-work has a long history, and more or less purely ornamental exercises in it appealed to a section of Victorian taste. Indeed, its practice was recommended (with full instructions) by *The Family Friend.* Admittedly, this periodical's preference for what it rashly termed 'a recently introduced branch of the art', gilt-leather-work, may be set aside in favour of the Victorian 'oak-coloured leather-work', which is, perhaps, rather less difficult to find nowadays. Considering that 'thousands have admired and practised that excellent and easy method of imitating old oaken carvings', it is impressive to reflect how relatively little of their work has come down to us.

Perhaps caskets and wall-brackets have stood as good a chance of survival as any, not counting such *tours-de-force* as have found permanent homes in public collections. One contemplates the 'Pattern Bracket – Vine Leaves and Grapes' (Fig. 54) with a slightly awed approval,

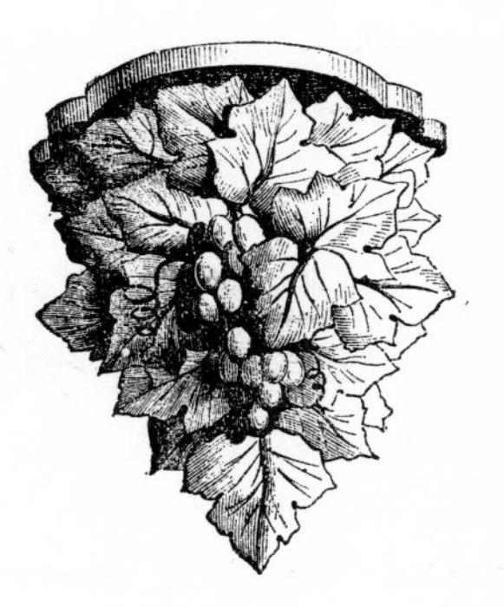

Fig. 54. Cut-leather-work Wall Bracket of the early 1850s. (From *The Family Friend*)

mitigated by wonder as to how on earth it was kept free from dust? Maybe, a proud creatrix cared for it herself. Some servants were *so* heavy-handed . . . . !

6

In passing, who has heard of 'The Great Eastern Lamp-Shade'? Though tolerably acquainted with Victoriana, I confess I had no ideas on the matter before that book by the Landells, previously noticed, came my way. There was, of course, no question about the *Great Eastern* herself. Still talked about fifty years after her launching, she was, in her day, the largest steamship afloat, with a gross tonnage of 18,195 tons. Designed by Isambard Kingdom Brunel, *The Great Eastern* was built in 1858. Hence she was still very much news when the Landells first put out their *Girl's Own Toy-maker*, and the *Great Eastern*'s laying of the first

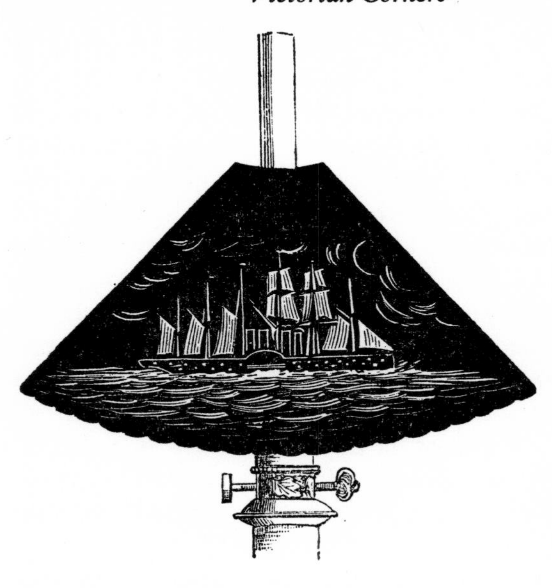

Fig. 55. Great Eastern Lamp-Shade, from *The Girl's Own Toy-Maker* (first published in 1860)

(successful) Atlantic cable would have kept her in later editions of the book, even if events were less easily outdated than they are nowadays.

It is a measure of the *Great Eastern*'s impact on the public fancy that such a triviality as a 'Great Eastern Lamp-shade' should have come into being. Here is a sterling instance of Victorian 'Do-it-Yourself' in its less exacting forms.

One cut out a lamp-shade 'in stout brown or other paper'; then made an outer casing in green-glazed cardboard, on which one drew a severely simplified silhouette of the ship, with appropriate wave-effects: all this being cut out wholly or partly, according to the nature of the detail. 'A few clouds and lights about the sky' were added to taste, and the whole finished off with a lining of tissue paper.

With a light inside – and one hopes that, with so much inflammable material, it was carefully placed – a pretty result was obtained. As the authors pointed out, a like technique was applicable to 'Groups of flowers, fruit, moonlight effects, waterfalls, birds, or animals', which, 'when executed with skill, have a very rich and beautiful effect'.

Note the gravity of the rider – 'when executed with skill' – in itself justifiable, yet somehow reflecting the admonitory side of Victorian 'Do-it-Yourself'. If things – even pressing flowers or sticking scraps in albums – were to be done at all, they should be done properly.

7

This admonitory note, so prevalent in Victorian books and the more 'serious' periodicals, found vent in the *Answers to Correspondents* columns which could be relied on as cheap space-fillers, and which now and again present us with literary tidbits. As one who, in younger days, had his share of running correspondence columns, and retains a sense of the technique involved, I marvel not only at what was printed, but at the phrasing of replies. Take *The Englishwoman's Domestic Magazine* about 1861. Here was a woman's magazine with nothing like the climate of women's magazines as we know them. Clearly the editor believed in keeping readers in order. *Notices to Correspondents* repay selective quotation. Some, presumably, are replies to genuine letters, others, probably, thought up in the office; but let us not discriminate. It is the *tone* that hits us. Who, in these latter days, would publish such an answer to 'JULIA FROST' as:

'No madam, it cannot be done. If you have a moustache growing on your upper lip you must bear it like – well, like a woman; and we know that the endurance of a woman is equal to anything. Consolation, however, may come to you in this form, perhaps – the dark-complexioned girls of Spain are thought, by all who have seen them, extremely beautiful, and upon *their* upper lips the downy hair is not unfrequently observed.'

Or again:

'FIX. – Are you quite sure you have not indulged in a little facetiousness when you talk about a wash for the hair, "purchased at a respectable chemist's", turning your hair "green, violet, and yellow"? . . . .'

'KATE. – Can we tell you the boundary-line which separates honest criticism from flattery? Can you tell us where matter ends and spirit begins? No! of course you cannot. Nobody can, perhaps never will, ambitious KATE . . . .'

'ELLEN should make quite sure that she wears easy boots. Bathing the feet in salt and water will harden them.'

'AMY ROBSART. – There is no doubt about Blondin's having crossed Niagara on a rope.'

(He did so in 1859, and an inner voice warns me that here is one possible fill-up.)

But to cap these extracts from sundry issues of *The Englishwoman's Domestic Magazine*, here is an enigmatic answer to one 'ETHEL MAY'.

'Your question is one which it would not be exactly discreet to answer in these columns: it is a question for a medical man to answer. But, touching the smoking of tobacco by women, we know it is practised extensively in Eastern lands, and even in England and Ireland, with more picturesque than sanitary effects.'

One subdues a wish to know more about 'ETHEL MAY'.

NINE

Victorian Lucky-Dip

'Old-fashioned? I should jolly well hope so! – Old and *Fashioned*.' WINSLOW RHODE

I

IT was about the turn of the reigns, from Victoria to Edward VII, that I became gramophone-conscious. Not that such things were new, though still a novelty in many homes; and the first to appear in our family circle was a brass-horned affair which brayed out its

Fig. 56. Modernities of 1897:– 'Excelsior Phonograph', Type A.T.; and a spring-driven H.M.V. Gramophone with up-to-date clockwork motor in place of the old hand-operated mechanism. (*Both in the Science Museum, South Kensington*)

music at my Uncle Swinfen's country-place at Weybridge in Surrey. That is to say, his then country-place, many years before he gave up Oatlands Lodge and bought Wood Norton, Evesham, from the Duc d'Orléans. (This, by the way, was the then Orléanist Pretender to the Throne of France, Philippe, Duc d'Orléans, nicknamed *gamelle*, whose indiscreet praise of

. TWO MR SMITHS: *Albert Smith* (1816–60), author, entertainer, friend of Charles Dickens. From an engraving (1847) by J. W. Cook after Charles Baugniet: and the same plate as later brought up to date and 'bearded'. And *Louis-Philippe, King of the French*, who as 'William Smith' fled to England in the Revolution of 1848. Engraving by James Thomson after Baron Gérard. (*Mr Winslow Rhode*)

16. Fashion-plate by L. Guerdet after Jules David from the *Englishwoman's Domestic Magazine*, October, 1861, with, in background, a romantically 'baronial' cabinet

an offensive caricature of Queen Victoria earned him the displeasure of the future King Edward VII).

But the time I have in mind was in or around the year when the Old Queen was laid to her long rest at Frogmore; and Uncle Swinfen, a prominent silk, was raised to the Bench: a time

Fig. 57. The Real Music of the Future: George du Maurier's prophetic drawing of voice recording (by phonograph), '*With Mr Punch's compliments and apologies to Mr Edison and Colonel Gouraud*,' in *Punch*, December 8, 1888. (By permission)

when it was rather stylish to have one of these talking machines. Anyhow, we all listened to the new toy, and the learned judge was heard to chuckle drily at recordings by Dan Leno, and one of Henry Lytton singing –

> 'When I marry Amelia, won't we have the dome
> Newly decorated and electro-plated . . . '

which last song (from *The Toreador*) was on disc in 1902, though the others could have been earlier.

Now that early models of the gramophone and its predecessor the phonograph are collectors' pieces, as are the more interesting records or cylinders associated with one or the other, it is worth emphasizing that (ignoring certain prototypes) their practical development on more or less familiar lines was well within the Victorian Age. In this sense, the phonograph dates back into the 1870s, the gramophone to 1894, the year of my birth. Thus when the

Fig. 58. Wonders of Science. The Electric Telegraph in the early 1850s (From *The Family Friend*)

Gramophone resounded in the drawing-room at Oatlands Lodge, we were quite in the movement.

Not that the gramophone or the still gawkier phonograph were much to look at in those days. Yet they and their predecessors have become the fossil-remains of a great and valuable industry's childhood. There was, as yet, little effort to mitigate the stark functionalism of the machine. Even so, attempts were not lacking to decorate other kinds of machinery. Back in the 1850s, an electric telegraph transmitter might be housed in a structure flanked with classic pilasters, and crowned with a kind of quasi-ecclesiastical belfry in the faltering neo-Gothic of the period.

It was at this point that it occurred to me to look-see what my tattered old copy of Haydn's *Dictionary of Dates*, the 1885 edition (Ward, Lock & Co.), had to say about phonography, and I was entranced by the final words of the following extract.

'Linear indentations are made by means of a pin in a sheet of tinfoil by speaking or singing: and from these casts may be taken. When these are placed upon the diaphragm of a telephone connected with revolving apparatus, the sounds may be reproduced with a weirdlike effect.'

'Weirdlike' is useful.

2

I may be a shade apt to miss the Apocalypse through worrying over a 'bus fare, but mention of Uncle Swinfen's gramophone somehow reminds me of one of my favourite toyshops – the other was in Putney – long since vanished from the neighbourhood of Finchley Road Station. How longingly I gazed at certain 'iron trains' in its window, and how eagerly were they greeted when, one birthday or Christmastide, those selfsame trains turned up in my parcels.

They were truly iron trains – of cast iron – the coaches, at least, being made in two halves joined together. The rear coach had those fascinating little observation windows, projecting from the sides of the guard's van; and the engine and tender (provocative of a riddle I was not supposed to enjoy) were both satisfactory. There was no track – 'railway lines' as I should have called them; and I never heard of any. Each item was weighty, coloured a sort of goldy reddish brown, and made a dull thud when dropped on the nursery floor. (This, by the way, was discouraged). They were my pride for many a year; but it was not until I was very much grown-up that I bought my car. It cost me eighteen pence.

My car had begun its career as a child's toy; it turned up in an antique shop, and if it dated from the early years of the twentieth century, I should not be surprised. Cars were then still

Fig. 59. Veteran car: a toy from the early years of the twentieth century (*ex coll. the Author*)

enough of a novelty to make one turn and stare after them as, emitting blue and noisome fumes, they chugged and honked along the streets. Horse-'bus drivers and cabbies made impolite noises at them, lashing out with that devastating wit for which 'bus drivers and cabbies were noted in those days.

'Come on, old Pilgrim's Progress!' shouted one of them to a bowed figure painfully crossing the road with a large bundle on his back. And 'Nah then, Guy Fawkes!' bawled another to a begoggled driver in a snorting contraption: none less than the learned judge earlier mentioned who, on occasion, chose to take the wheel.

Some remote small boy must have revelled in owning my little eight-inch long car, when it was an up-to-date plaything. It was all in the game if he cut a finger on a sharp metal edge. But by the time that car reached me, she was a distinctly old model. Her paint, a pillar-box red with a natty green line, had gone shabby. Steering column and wheel had vanished, as had the miniature driver and passenger who plugged into holes in the front seats. But, for all that, when I had her, that old crock still *worked.*

Beneath the body was a heavy fly-wheel, hung on spindles through holes in the under-carriage. The spindles passed between and engaged the car-wheels. One could wind a string round the end of a spindle, pull it smartly away – when the fly-wheel revolved, the car-wheels turned, and the car ambled forward with exemplary zeal. Or in reverse, according to the way one had wound on the string.

I gave up that car ages ago, and rather wish I hadn't. She had the compelling charm of the utterly useless.

3

Memory, swiftest of all chariots, here impulsively drops me back into the past in time, and in place into kind G. A. Storey's studio at the top of his tall house in Broadhurst Gardens. 'Hougoumont', its name in those days, struck an individual note in South Hampstead.

It was in this studio that I was privileged to have my first sight of that remarkable early self-portrait, which, painted when Storey was nineteen, was brought out in his latter days to general applause. When my father and I were praising its sympathy, the now old Storey quietly remarked: 'I was in love when I painted it.' And he met other laudations in similar words, voiced with the deepest sincerity. Indeed, his life-long devotion to Mrs Storey was reflected over and over again in his art.

But it is not so much with Storey, as former Pre-Raphaelite, later of the St John's Wood Clique, but as author of the gossiping *Sketches from Memory* (Chatto & Windus, 1899) to whom my present mood inclines. For in that book, Storey tells a tale of the once-celebrated author, entertainer and friend of Dickens, Albert Smith.

Having decided (as he said) to cut a more dignified figure in future, Albert Smith went to a dance, where one of his partners remarked the beauty of a flower in his button-hole.

"Do you like it?" said he. "I raised it myself in a blacking-bottle on the roof."

It is a good little anecdote, and it invites contemplation of what has been happily called the law of coincidence. For Mr Smith had a nephew who became my Uncle Swinfen, who bought Wood Norton of the great-grandson of Louis Philippe, who, when he ceased to be King of the French in 1848, fled to England under the pseudonym of – 'Mr Smith'.

There was, of course, not the slightest connexion, but the pattern so formed is – dare I say it? – intriguing.

4

Whether there is any underlying association between Albert Smith's alleged blacking-bottle (which inevitably recalls Dickens's unhappy boyhood) and the miscellany of bygones to which we are coming is left to the reader's imagination. Bygones – an astute curator once suggested 'Bygoings' as an alternative for items not quite in the bygone category[42] – bygones is a useful term for things out-dated without as yet being antique, with a considerable reference to utilitarian items. For example, while pottering in an antique shop not so long ago, I noticed one of the old cast-iron coffee-mills, in full working order, with its little drawer under, its maker's brass label with the Royal Arms, and the holed flanges at its base for screwing it to the kitchen dresser – as I remember these things in my childhood. Nor let me forget the shining armoury of dish-covers, and those rich-toned copper vessels, pans and moulds, sometime serviceable, later discarded, now in renewed demand as decoration. If some such items be pre-Victorian, the mass of old examples presumably dates from somewhere in the longest

[42] C. I. Gardner: 'Bygoings', letter in *The Museums Journal*, June 1936.

reign. Modern versions of brass or copper 'helmet' scuttles, echoing what have become traditional types, are numerous, though old examples are not lacking.

Which again reminds me of that Victorian accessory the speaking-tube, used as what is now called intercom in a good many homes and offices, and prevalent in doctors' houses for parleying with agitated beings intent on winkling the good man out of bed in the small hours. (It was some form of speaking-tube that originated the pleasing vulgarism 'on the blower'.) There was a speaking-tube between above-stairs and basement in our house at West Hampstead. One removed the stopper-cum-whistle, blew down the tube thus sounding the whistle in place at t'other end in the kitchen. Such was the theory (which, until I was warned off, appealed to me), though an incautiously powerful blast had been known to shoot the whistle out into the middle of the kitchen.

It may have been this occupational hazard that my father had in mind when I asked him what happened to the water when it drained away from the fitted wash-basin in the bathroom? (I *had* seen a fitted wash-basin before, but this one attracted me). My father's reply, to the effect that the water came out in the kitchen, 'all over Mrs Spiring', so interested me that I dropped his tooth-brush down the waste pipe, without any such gratifying result.

This must have happened in 1898, when we had newly arrived in Priory Road; when the Storeys and the Seymour Lucases were living in neighbouring roads, when nobody had yet dreamed of placing a tablet on Kate Greenaway's house in Frognal[43]; and when elderly Mr and Mrs Spiring, he an old and trusted artist's model, were 'doing' for us until a permanent staff arrived. Such accommodations were not, presumably are not, unusual in the art world, and quite often worked well enough. Domestic arrangements apart, it ensured an artist having a model on hand at a moment's notice.

Fig. 60. Two pottery peppers, one a typical fairing of vaguely 'Kate Greenaway' aspect. (*Belonging to Mrs M. Maynard*)

[43] Not that I ever met her, though that distinction fell to the lot of my old friend Gladys Storey, OBE, G. A. Storey's daughter.

5

Which again puts me in mind of an item of Victoriana not easily come by nowadays, should one happen to need such a thing. Behind our Priory Road home, my father had built out a studio, designed by the same Sydney W. Lee whom we met earlier. It was heated by a tubular 'Tortoise' coke-stove, was full of old oak and armour, and had in its west wall a seventeenth-century oak door. This opened on to a small glory-hole, part models' changing room, part storage for frames and canvases.

But there was something else in that windowed recess: a something which halted me in my tracks, until I grew used to it. Prone on the floor lay a contorted brown man wearing a ragged pair of red hose or, an you will, 'tights'. The head, expressionless, was loose, and some of the fingers were missing – one of them turned up years later in a box of oddments. It was beautifully fashioned and jointed, with an indentation where the nail would be in life.

Coming upon this silent horror, which had the air of an assassinated mummy, I stopped, reached for my father's forefinger, and fearfully asked him what the thing was? When he good-humouredly told me that it was a man who had died and turned to wood, I recoiled. But before anyone prates about traumas and the like, let me add my whole-hearted belief that the sole effects of my father's idle jest – for he was extremely kind to me – were to rob me of all fear of lay figures and to strengthen my already budding sense of dramatic situation.

For that is what the wooden man was: an old lay figure, used for drapery painting and odds and ends not requiring a 'live' pose. It was lifesized, and in general construction belonged to a ball-jointed type known at least as early as the seventeenth century. (Adriaen van Ostade shows one in *The Artist at his Easel* (1633), at Dresden). Like-fashioned mannikins of wood, on a small scale, are still obtainable new from artists' colourmen. They, too, have a pedigree, as witness the sculptor Roubiliac's 'small lay-man': a jointed mannikin, with its own wardrobe

Fig. 61. 'Sixty-three hours before Receiving Day. Brilliant sunshine. Jones the model very busy. Typical studio of the period, from a Fred Roe sequence in *Fun*, March 11, 1891.

of male and female wigs and dresses, in the London Museum. Which does not imply that our man who 'turned to wood' was as old as that one; but Victorian it was and not too late Victorian either.

Fig. 62. The Professional Model with stock poses. *Defiance*, 'the 'and's on the beard'. Note lay-figure in background. From a 'Jassef' Sullivan sequence in *The British Working Man*. (*Fun* Office, 1878)

6

Talk of that old coffee-mill, a few sections back, awakens other metallic echoes, among them the clatter of Victorian plate and cutlery. Such as discern few virtues in Victorian silver, unless it be for its phases of entertaining exuberance on the one hand, or the plainer 'utility' forms on the other, may have little to say in its praise. But this attitude is already out of favour with many, and, as always, separation of the sheep from the goats may at least induce tolerance.

To give a simple example, the familiar 'fiddle-pattern' spoon and fork, which appearing early in the nineteenth century were to hold their own right through the Victorian Age, varied a good deal in quality. Quite apart from 'king pattern' and other variations of design, we very soon notice that, so far as looks are concerned, some 'fiddle-pattern' items are easier on the eye than are others. Well chosen, such things are satisfying. There may, too, be other points of interest.

Idly handling a large 'fiddle-pattern' ladle in a shop, I noticed, engraved on its butt, a crest ensigned with an earl's coronet. The engraving was nicely done, doubtless in character with that on my lord's battery of silverware. But this ladle was not silver but nickel; and whether it was meant for lesser occasions or, maybe, for use below stairs, was not for me to decide. And if, here and there, I linger before lesser items, rather than the more stupendous creations of Rundell, Bridge & Rundell, the Garrards, Elkington, or Hunt and Roskell – the last inseparably associated with that amazing trophy *The Outram Shield* (1862) – it is because, of their nature, such *tours-de-force* reflect an exclusive as distinct from a popular trend.

Not that this argument can be carried far. It has been plausibly suggested that the very ostentation of certain Victoriana is once again attractive (as it certainly was in its day-spring), and is now more tolerable than the conscious mannerisms of Gothic Revivalists and other purists of the age. In plain fact, Classicists, Gothic Revivalists, Morris, the Pre-Raphaelites,

Aesthetes, Academics, and Decadents all mirrored, when they did not create, facets of Victorian culture. That Burges's *Cadmus* cabinet (elsewhere discussed) is in its own mood as typical of one trend of Victorian taste as (say) the ornate exuberance of *The Queen's Vase, Ascot* (1847), is of another, stresses the essential Victorianism of both.

TEN

Baronialism

'. . . the "Pocklington Arms." Such a shield it is! Such quarterings! Howard, Cavendish, De Ros, De la Zouche, all mingled together.' W. M. THACKERAY

I

Two men were talking in a railway carriage.

Said one: he was on to a good thing. Building small 'ouses in the suburbs – nothing common – small 'ouses with a bit of sham timbering and stained glass: baronial 'alls at £40 a year.

That, in my own paraphrase, is the tale as it reached me, half a lifetime ago. Whether it

Fig. 63. 'She will come to-morrow': wood-engraving by C. Gray after George Cattermole in which the designer has given full play to his Gothicness. From *The Old Curiosity Shop* (1840–1)

Fig. 64. Its design inspired by an armorial gate-post, a mid-Victorian cast-iron Door porter, H. $15\frac{1}{8}$ ins.

reflected an actual experience or was one of those stories which pass from mouth to mouth, quoted or misquoted, like the 'curate's egg' joke from *Punch*, is beyond my discovery. But the trend to 'baronial 'alls' is important enough to be dealt with here.

In a stylistic sense 'baronialism' was a reaction to the urge to rediscover and realize the past that has already been noted in the Victorian world of literature, paint and design. As so often happens, such movements have their rise in study or studio, spread gradually outwards until their last faint ripples are absorbed in the enormous reaches of popular misunderstanding. In this book, Victorian Gothic, good or bad, is treated as a convenient unit. Victorian Gothic brick houses – variegated brick, maybe – for the most part ordinary dwellings with sash-windows in their pointed lights, a mock-Gothic corbel or so, and a certain spikyness of roof-line; such, varying mainly in size, became accepted as a part of the scheme of things. One characteristic example, barge-boarded, gabled and with immense lancets in its pointed-capped tower, where I visited when very young, had its extensive drawing-room hung with dark old paintings of the great Duke of Marlborough's victories, in allusion to the chatelaine's descent from one of his officers. Still more ambitious, if not necessarily larger, architectural schemes resulted in such noteworthy domestic structures as Burges's 'Tower House', already noticed, and so upwards until the vast labyrinth of Alfred Waterhouse's Eaton Hall (1867–80) rose to demonstrate its shortcomings as a palace out of dreamland. Sundry lugubrious hospital buildings, suggestive of a cross between medieval *châteaux* and one of the grimmer public sanitary services; *plus* Sir Gilbert Scott's Midland Grand Hotel at St Pancras Station, which proved just how nearly a railway terminus might approach, without actually becoming, a palatial Gothic guildhall, demonstrated other facets of 'baronialism', among which the 'new'

17. *An old Baptistery*, water-colour by George Cattermole in similar vein to his richly Gothic illustrations in Dickens's *Old Curiosity Shop*. Compare Fig. 63 (*Author*)

18. W. J. Moore, as Marlborough (Masque of Painters, 1887).
(*Photo. Disdéri & Co.*)

19. Artists in costume (left to right): Charles Green, RI; Fred Roe (the latter in Masque of Painters, 1887).
(*Photos. Disdéri & Co., Valentine Blanchard*)

20. Interior dating from 1889 (Sydney W. Lee, FRIBA), since destroyed, Putney Hill, Surrey. Note 'Abbotsford' type chair in foreground among authentic antiques. (*Photo. John Pain-Clark*)

Houses of Parliament were, of course, pre-eminent. But it is not with these that our present interest lies; save in so far as worked stones, removed from Barry and Pugin's Parliament buildings in the course of repairs, have travelled here, there and everywhere, and may even be found ekeing out a modest retirement, in suburban front gardens.

Despite the alluring more-Gothic-than-Gothic of George Cattermole's fancy, one must beware of creating an impression that every inhabitant of the less palatial kind of Victorian Gothic dwelling-house was conscious of living Gothically, or in, as it were, a profane counterpart of the Oxford Movement. In many, the lace curtains, the prints after Landseer or Lady Butler, the staid Victorian furniture, not forgetting the proverbial aspidistras in art pots, and the brass or brass-knobbed bedsteads, held undisputed sway. But, when in season, antiques began to be distinguished from the quasi-antique, it became apparent that whereas 'Abbotsford' furniture might be at ease in a Victorian Gothic setting, an authentic Gothic chest – then still to be picked up cheaply by the perceptive – looked rather odd. And so, led to a great extent by artists' treatment of their studios, connoisseurs and, way after them, the public began to discern virtues in a different type of background. That, in course of time, this was dissipated in a welter of wilful quaintness and roguish old-oakery does not cheapen the merit of its original impulse.

Even so, innocent amusement can be had from roaming suburban streets and noting here, the faced-on planks which should be solid beams; there, the disturbingly coloured glass, in which traces of *Art Nouveau* mingle with quasi-armorial shield-shapes, and the pargeting of gables is worked with what, in happier circumstances, might be coats-of-arms. When these last are used as a repeat-pattern, one to each house in a row, a passing antiquary may be excused for recalling one of George du Maurier's *Punch* jokes in 1890: that of a charming lady instructing a harassed architect about a new house. 'I want it to be nice and baronial, Queen Anne and Elizabethan, and all that, kind of quaint and Nuremburgy you know – regular Old English, with French windows opening on to the lawn, and Venetian blinds, and sort of Swiss balconies, and a loggia.'

2

Destruction has overtaken more than the Victorian Gothic Villa; it has also struck the Tudoresque or neo-Jacobean house of superior design, of which part of Avenue House at Finchley is happily a surviving instance. As we have seen, these later features of Avenue House date from 1884, about which time there was a renewed taste for such architectural exercises. One of the best I knew, a red-brick neo-Jacobean gabled structure of 1889, with terra-cotta mullions and caryatids besides elaborate internal fittings, some of them antique, has vanished without trace from Putney Hill within relatively recent years.

This, it is true, had rather more of a 'manor-house' than a 'baronial' effect, but of its kind it was dignified and aesthetically endearing. Slightly more baronial, perhaps, was another house, a mile away. This was in a mixed style, features of which included some neat little Norman pillars flanking the front-door steps; and an Oak Room (with good modern panelling), in its inglenook decorative paintings by Seymour Lucas of a reclining *Touchstone* on one side of the hearth, and of a lass on the other. But what most readily caught the eye was a small circular head of the owner, set in the panelling above the inglenook. This, too, was from Lucas's brush; and as Lucas (among others) had a certain taste for 'costume' portraits, in which his sitters wore the dress of other days, the worthy Mr W's shrewd, side-whiskered face appeared above an Elizabethan ruff, provoking irresistible comparisons with Dog Toby. It was a good portrait, all the same; and, before identifying 'costume' portraiture too exclusively with the later nineteenth century, we may as well reflect that it had been resorted to by many earlier artists, among whom Rembrandt, Reynolds, Gainsborough are obvious choices.

3

Among the lesser evidences of what, in this book, is styled 'baronialism' might be numbered certain metal trophies, which did something to atone for a deficiency of ancient arms and armour.

My initial experience of such objects was in one of those tall, grey-brick South Kensington terrace-houses with classic porticos, some sixty years ago. In the sense of this book, there was nothing 'baronial' about that interior; it was comfortable, well-to-do, commonplace, dull. But in the hall hung a pair of these factitious trophies of arms which, at the time, perversely intrigued me.

On ovals covered in plush (or some such material) was mounted a lilliputian armoury in cast iron, with a wee helmet over a curly, pageant shield, from which sprouted a bristling array of swords, spears, haldberds, flanked by a pair of extremely small gauntlets. By casting the helmet in halves, and distributing them between the two trophies, that sense of symmetry, dear to Victorian eyes, was achieved. Neither helmet nor gauntlets, nor anything else had any practical function whatsoever; nor was their stylistic period anything other than that known to senior collectors as 'bulgeydingo'. Such trophies were, in short, ornaments (if that word be permissible). Now and again, at long intervals, odd bits of cast metal, noticed in smaller antique shops, have struck me as having possibly come from broken-up examples of these egregious quasi-antiques. When they were made in the nineteenth century I simply don't know, but if anyone tells me that there is a look of the 1850s or '60s about some of them, I'm in no mood for argument. Of course, real, man-sized armours were available if wanted, to say nothing of arms, halberds had as much decorative appeal as any other, not to say loose items, helmets, breastplates, etc., which looked well on a wall. The demand for such things in an average home was slight, which left more for the artists' studios and the homes of antiquaries. There were, however, two drawbacks: such things were a nuisance to clean, and not a few of them, including the most romantic, turned out to be creations rather than antiquities. And if one wished to have avowedly modern copies of Gothic armours or of almost any weapon one wanted, a well-known firm made and supplied such things, which could be selected at leisure from an attractively illustrated catalogue.

4

While on the subject of metalwork, certain aspects of brass ware can be fitted into our baronial outlook. From about the second half of the nineteenth century comes a quantity of objects:

Fig. 65. In Renaissance style: a late nineteenth-century brass handbell.

Fig. 66. In fifteenth-century style, a late Victorian oak Bookslide.

inkstands, pen-trays, paper-knives, match-boxes, handbells, and so forth, with strong suggestions of Renaissance influence in their cast ornament. Even a pair of quasi-Elizabethan snuffers, its arms cast with caryatids, has come my way – though this may have had a longer Victorian past. At its best, this neo-Renaissance brass ware is not unattractive, as with a handbell familiar to me any time these seventy years, and which may have been more or less new in 1890. Its ornament of Romayne heads in roundels, surrounded by grotesques, is an attractive exercise based on sixteenth-century motifs. And I recall with affection a brass ink-pot, fashioned as a grotesque head on tiny feet, which clearly owed inspiration to an Italian model of similar period. It stood on my Grannie Lee's Davenport, which had curly, beast-headed supports, a row of real drawers on one side of its carcase, and a row of false drawers on the other. As John Gloag would tell us: the Davenport, which took various forms, harks back to the late eighteenth century, when the firm of Gillow made one, 'described as a desk', for a certain Captain Davenport.[44]

Loudon in 1833 stated that these 'drawing-room writing-cabinets used by ladies' were called '*Devonports*' [*sic*] 'from the inventor's name', the significance of which depends a good deal on what was meant by 'inventor'. That Captain Davenport was a customer of Gillow's is established fact; as is the detail that, having begun in a Regency mood, Davenports adapted themselves to changes of vogue, some later versions being not unpleasingly suggestive of a sixteenth–seventeenth century atmosphere. It might be excessive to claim even for these any marked 'baronial' leanings.

The same reservation applies to sundry Gothicisms in woodwork, the inspiration of which is more directly ecclesiastical than baronial, influenced in many cases by the Catholic Revival in the Church of England. Thus, shops in university cities would supply the serious reading man with such items as an extending book-slide of carved and pierced oak, creditably sug-

[44] John Gloag: *A Short Dictionary of Furniture* (George Allen & Unwin Ltd.).

gestive of what a fifteenth-century book-slide would have looked like had such things been known medievally. Various other items, from letter-racks to full-scale furniture, were available to such as were open to Middle-Ages enchantments, and it should be made clear that by no means all of these sprang from *after* the onset of the Oxford Movement in 1833.

One item of furniture which doubtless received an impetus from the Movement was the (so-called) 'Glastonbury Chair': a folding type of which older examples exist, but which is most numerously represented by revivals of Victorian vintage, such as are still found in churches, and, at any rate in my time, on the master's dais in schoolrooms. Many were plain to severity, but carved examples occur. Millais drew one in an illustration for the first instalment of Harriet Martineau's story 'Sister Anna's Probation' in *Once a Week* (1862). Antique examples of sixteenth- and seventeenth-century date are known, but the name 'Glastonbury Chair' has no better authority than an example (at Wells), described and figured in Henry Shaw's *Specimens of Ancient Furniture* (1836), plate IX, as 'The Abbot's Chair, Glastonbury, Date, the time of Henry 8th'. As though to make sure of its origin, this curious chair bears inscriptions carved on its back and arms, some reading 'IOHANES ARTHURUS' and 'MONACHUS GLASTONIE', which were held to settle the matter. But the name of the martyred Abbot of Glastonbury in 1539 was Richard Whiting; and though some authorities, such as Francis Bond, have assigned the chair to *circa* 1530, others have favoured a much later date for it.

5

Among the occasions on which Victorians did their best to enter into the spirit of the past (as they understood that rather vague phrase) were those when fancy dress was worn. Naturally, not all fancy dress was historical, or even pretended to be anything other than fanciful. But a study of the historical type (so to call it) is amusing as well as instructive, and that there were close links between it and the theatre is obvious.

When (in *Pickwick*) the poetically disposed Mr Snodgrass attended Mrs Leo Hunter's fancy-dress 'dejeune', it seemed entirely in order for him to don 'blue satin trunks and cloak, white silk tights and shoes', which plus a large ruff and Greek helmet, were recognized as 'the regular, authentic, every-day costume of a Troubadour, from the earliest ages down to the time of their final disappearance from the face of the earth'.

That in this, as in many other ways, Dickens was far from being the caricaturist he is supposed to have been by those unversed in his age, is proven by pictorial records of the antiquarianly disastrous fancy dresses too often worn, by royalty downwards. When Thackeray makes his George Savage Fitz-Boodle[45] attend a fancy ball, to which, 'the poems of Scott being at that time all the fashion', guests went in appropriate character, he creates an immediate impression of expensive anachronisms.

Such ingenuous staginess was in time challenged though, like the Merry Monarch, it was long a'dying – if indeed it has ever done so. Old photographs reveal its persistence alongside more credible effects which, largely arising in artists' studios, complemented and encouraged a greater realism on the stage. It is thus with no surprise that we find Henry Irving calling in Seymour Lucas to design dresses for his productions of *Henry VIII* or *Ravenswood*; or

[45] *The Fitz-Boodle Papers* first appeared in 1842.

Charles Green designing an effective late sixteenth-century *ensemble* for his own use at the first of the balls held by the Royal Institute of Painters in Water-Colours in the 1880s. Furthermore, Green not only wore the dress but himself arranged the pose in a suitable Old Masterish style, when he was photographed by Valentine Blanchard of Regent Street.

This particular tendency to a creative use of the camera is traceable back to about the 1860s. Then David Wilkie Wynfield (otherwise 'Winkie' Wynfield), a painter-member of the St John's Wood Clique, recognized the possibilities of this kind of camera-work,[46] which in the '80s received an impetus from such outstanding events as the Masque of Painters at the R.I. Galleries in May, 1887, with its *tableaux vivants*.

Enormous trouble was taken to make this occasion an artistic success, and in one case, at least, authentically antique costume was worn; and when the Prince and Princess of Wales and other royalties arrived, they were received by a guard of honour of halberdiers. The Prince (later King Edward VII) expressed his gratification with the tableaux to Sir James D. Linton (then PRI) desiring him to transmit the same to each of those who took part. In addition to groups, getting on for 150 photographs of individual participants in the RI balls, 'and taking part in the Tableaux & Gavotte before their RHHS' were made and exhibeted by Disdéri & Co., of Brook Street, Hanover Square.

And the selfsame year (1887) was published the fifth edition of Ardern Holt's *Fancy Dresses Described*, with chromo and other plates, providing a large number of easy recipes as to how to appear on the dance floor as Mary, Queen of Scots, or even Eve (very decent in white India muslin, with fig-leaf pocket out of which peeps a serpent with emerald eyes). Not but what my own eye might have been more on a lass who chose to go dressed as a Hornet; but that is in passing.

6

A minor point of interest in connexion with old photographs by professionals is a tendency for them to be glorified by, if not the Royal Arms, at least somebody's arms or what looked like such, hinting at noble patronage. When nothing else suggested itself the device of a buckled garter might, properly or otherwise, be brought into play; and there may occur emblems suggestive of private armorials.

Similarly the painted back-cloths against which sitters were posed are worth noting as much for their factitious realism as for their not infrequently Otrantoesque, even baronial, fancy. I have beside me a photograph of a small boy of 1896, wearing white dress and large white, feathered hat, posed on what could almost be a carved oak Abbotsford chair, against a painted cloth suggestive of a window with an achievement of arms leaded into it. Actually the device is non-heraldic and therefore accommodated a wide range of sitters; but the general effect of an ancestral hall is maintained.

Which reminds me that the nearest I have ever been to achieving even the similitude of an heritable dignity was when, in 1895, I was taken to be photographed by a famous firm, which, about that time, glorified their mounts with an earl's coronet, impressed in gilt below the portrait. Had it been over, not under, the effect would have been still more flattering.

[46] Helmut Gernsheim: *Masterpieces of Victorian Photography* (Arts Council, 1951), pp. 22–3. Wynfield's photography influenced that of the celebrated Mrs Cameron.

Fig. 67. Armorial Moods: (L) The Baroque Tradition: Book–plate of Thomas Philip, Earl de Grey (1781–1859); (R) The Gothic Revival: Book–plate of John Frederick (Campbell), 1st Earl Cawdor (1790–1860).

7

When one contemplates the slender grounds on which some folk laid claim to ancestral honours and ancient descent, the otherwise trifling matter of the previous paragraph becomes symbolical. In general, the Victorian Age was intensely conscious of pomp and circumstance, rank and condition, with a full, if by no means always accurate, appreciation of heraldry, titles, and vast family trees, some of the more romantic of which are still not as dead as they should be. Not that everyone cared for such things. Sturdy beings there were (with no nonsense about them, sir!) who openly contempted such gewgaws, though the number of those who valued nobility of rank and descent was far more extensive. That a sizeable proportion of such well-affected folk should themselves aspire to distinguished connexions or origins, followed as a matter of course.

To poke innuendoes at genuine honours and authentic descents, in whatever walk of life they occur, is no part of my purpose. The sixteenth-century labourer who willed that he be buried 'amongst my ancestors'[47] had no less a sense of communion with the rock from which he was hewn than had my lord, reflecting on how many more noble corpses could be accommodated in an inconveniently crowded family vault. But there were others whose regard for such matters took the practical form of matching family ambition and personal status on genealogical grounds – or what they believed to be such. In his Fitz-Boodle (whose family had 'held the estate of Boodle ever since the reign of Henry II', or so he said, and which on the like authority had 'refused a peerage any time these two hundred years') Thackeray knowingly satirized one of the various aspects of this brand of snobbery. 'How long the shadows of the antlers are on the wainscot, and the armour of Rollo Fitz-Boodle looks in the sunset as if it were emblazoned with rubies', is a romantic Fitz-Boodleism with factual parallels.

[47] 'North Country Wills' in *The Ancestor*, No. IV, January 1903, p. 103.

Fig. 68. Armorial Moods: Severely orthodox, for William Courthope (1808–66) Somerset Herald, and Editor of *Peerages.*

That there were families entitled to distinction of birth, descent, or title; theirs by moral right as well as by the more arduous process of established fact, is beyond cavil. But others there were whose enthusiasm, battened on in certain instances by unworthy advisers, deluded them into advancing claims which found their way into current works of reference. When (as in one case) a non-existent Countship of the Holy Roman Empire was called into shadowy being, the pinchbeck glittered enticingly.

Which, of course, has no bearing at all on Thackeray's George Bumpsher, Esquire, who 'does not sport a coronet and supporters upon his London plate and carriages'; though 'his country-house is emblazoned all over with those heraldic decorations'. For the worthy Bumpsher is truly a Count, if not of the Empire. 'He puts on an order when he goes abroad, and is Count Bumpsher of the Roman States – which title he purchased from the late Pope (through Prince Polonia the banker) for a couple of thousand scudi.' That, by the way, was written in 1848.

Not for me the ostentation of coronet or supporters in my modestly 'baronial' home on London's Northern Heights. But other things I claim, and with reasonable pride: among them, personal encounter with a venerable artist who had seen Turner plain, and to whom that mighty genius had long ago been kind.

INDEX

(References are to page numbers, except in the case of half-tone plates (*pl.*)
Illustrations are indicated in *italic* type.)